The Women's Revolution

Praise for *The Women's Revolution*

'Many have heard that the February Revolution began on International Women's Day. But rarely if ever has the story been told of women's lengthy, persistent and pivotal contribution to the fuller history of the Russian Revolution and of the Bolshevik Party in particular. Nor has the centrality of working-class feminism to that contribution been so thoroughly examined. In a richly detailed, absorbing account, Judy Cox reveals just that, making one wonder how the courage, brilliance and sheer number of women who helped change the course of history could ever have been missed in the first place!'

– SUE FERGUSON, associate professor, Wilfrid Laurier University

'This is a story of women fighting at barricades, of women theorising capitalism, of women robbing trains, and women smuggling weapons to fight the Tsar. Judy Cox has recovered for us not a narrative of "achievements" by "exceptional" women, but rather the more important history of how ordinary women, with revolutionary intentionality, fought, and nearly won, against capital. They are the true foremothers of feminism for the 99%.'

– TITHI BHATTACHARYA, *Feminism for the 99%*

'In *The Women's Revolution, 1905-1917*, Judy Cox places women at the centre of revolutionary organising, agitation and leadership in Russia. Her lively narrative ties Russian women's activism to that of other women in the European revolutionary tradition. Cox's vivid accounts of women's contributions at all levels of the Bolshevik Party organisation turn the table on those histories that marginalise women revolutionaries.'

– BARBARA C. ALLEN, *Leaflets of the Russian Revolution: Socialist Organizing in 1917*

'*The Women's Revolution* is an important reminder of the key role women played in the Russian Revolution of 1917. From Nadezhda Krupskaya to Alexandra Kollontai, women not only strategised about how to overturn the Tsarist regime and build a communist society, but also theorised and attempted to put into practice how such a new society could rid itself of entrenched misogyny.'

– SARA R. FARRIS, *In the Name of Women's Rights: The Rise of Femonationalism*

The Women's Revolution: Russia 1905–1917

Judy Cox

Haymarket Books
Chicago, Illinois

First published in Great Britain in 2017 by Counterfire.

This edition published in 2019 by
Haymarket Books
P.O. Box 180165
Chicago, IL 60618
773-583-7884
www.haymarketbooks.org
info@haymarketbooks.org

ISBN: 978-1-60846-784-6

Distributed to the trade in the US through Consortium Book
Sales and Distribution (www.cbsd.com) and internationally
through Ingram Publisher Services International
(www.ingramcontent.com).

This book was published with the generous support of
Lannan Foundation and Wallace Action Fund.

Special discounts are available for bulk purchases by
organizations and institutions. Please call 773-583-7884 or
email info@haymarketbooks.org for more information.

Cover design by Jamie Kerry.

Library of Congress Cataloging-in-Publication data
is available.

Entered into digital printing March, 2021

Contents

List of Illustrations

In memory of Jessica Cox (1961-2006)
and all the other disobedient daughters of history.

Introduction: The train

When Lenin arrived at the Finland Station in April 1917 he had already decided that the February Revolution could not be the end of the Russian Revolution. He was committed to fighting for a second, socialist revolution. That much, many socialists know. If pressed, we might recall that he was not alone on the famous sealed train, that his closest collaborator Grigory Zinoviev was with him. Karl Radek might also come into the picture – after all, he later wrote an account of the journey – and of course, there was the ever-loyal Nadezhda Krupskaya, Lenin's wife, and Inessa Armand, another of Lenin's closest collaborators. It might seem more surprising that Krupskaya and Armand were not the only female passengers.

Zlata Lilina Zinovieva was also on board. She had joined the Russian Social Democratic and Labour Party (RSDLP) in 1902, becoming a member of the Bolshevik faction the following year. She was active in the 1905 Revolution in St Petersburg and joined Lenin in exile with her husband Grigory Zinoviev. Together they became two of Lenin's closest allies during some eight years of exile. Zlata Lilina went on to be a key party activist in 1917. Another female passenger was Olga Ravich. She had joined the RSDLP in 1903 and four years later she was arrested after taking part in a Bolshevik-organised bank raid in Tiflis. She had also been married to Zinoviev, but by 1917 they were divorced. She too continued to be a respected and active party member and became a well-regarded writer after the revolution.

Lenin was at the heart of the Bolshevik Party. He was central to steering the party away from compromise and betrayal in April 1917 and to seizing power in October. But he was not alone. The women who shared his exile did not confine themselves to mending stockings and making the tea. They were Marxist revolutionaries who were committed to the emancipation of the working class. They all went on to play important roles in the revolutionary regime, becoming delegates to congresses and members of key committees. Yet today, it is hard to find any references to Zlata Lilina or to Olga at all, never mind to discover what they thought, what they argued or how they contributed to Lenin's perspective in the course of the revolution. Krupskaya and Armand are more prominent but tend to be seen purely as Lenin's helpers, transmitting his words to the wider world.

Lenin was certainly a towering figure of 1917 but at every stage of the revolution there were women debating, theorising and organising alongside him. While he is still either reviled or worshipped as the architect of the socialist revolution, the women close to him have been relegated to the shadows.

Section One
Revolutionary Times

1. Where are the women?

Women have been written out of all aspects of the Russian Revolution by historians of left and right, of East and of West. The dominant narrative of the revolution in the West portrays the Bolshevik Party as an organisation of iron-willed male fanatics who seized power behind the backs of the working class. Women had no role to play in this macho coup. In Stalinist histories, there was only room for the two great men who created the Soviet Union: Lenin and Stalin. Women were airbrushed out of leading roles, just as was Leon Trotsky.

Historians more sympathetic to the Bolsheviks have been little better. Elena Stasova was a Bolshevik leader willing and able to take orders, energetic, fearless and devoted to revolutionary politics. She was a staunch ally of Lenin and his wife Krupskaya in the underground movement, and she later served on key party committees. She served as the secretary to the Bolshevik Party Central Committee throughout 1917. Stasova was such a powerful figure that she was nicknamed 'Absolute', yet in Alexander Rabinowitch's well-regarded 400-page book, *The Bolsheviks Come to Power*,[1] she is literally reduced to a footnote.

Historians taking a more social approach have tended to relegate women to the unskilled and less organised sections of the workforce, and leave them there. These women workers may have set the revolution in motion with their riots for 'bread and herrings', but they quickly retreated back into the shadows to let the men take over the serious business of taking power. Richard Stites argues in *The Women's Liberation Movement in Russia* that women do not appear in histories of 1917 because they did not walk the corridors of power or make the important decisions. Therefore, he continues, 'there is no sense in trying to magnify the role played by the female half of the population during 1917'.[2]

Recent contributions on the Russian Revolution have been less dismissive of women's role. Women from a range of oppositional political organisations feature in China Miéville's 2017 *October: The Story of the Russian Revolution*.[3] Tariq Ali's 2017 *The Dilemmas of Lenin*[4] devotes a chapter to women, in which he discusses the theoretical roots of Marxists' analysis of women's oppression and debates around the family and sexuality. Curiously, however, the role played by women during the events of 1917 is not developed in his narrative.

The handful of female Bolsheviks who are remembered today derive their status exclusively from their relationships to important men. They are almost invariably described in a series of stereotypes. The women are tragic, neglected wives, glamorous and sexy beauties or shrewish spinsters. A biography of Nadezhda Krupskaya was titled *Bride of the Revolution*,[5] as if only her marriage to Lenin could excite readers' interest. Inessa Armand is remembered as Lenin's glamorous friend and possible lover.

The language used to describe socialist women is frequently steeped in sexist assumptions. Women revolutionaries are judged by how sexually attractive they were. Ugly old maids and irritating mothers-in-law are dismissed while the physical attributes of beautiful women are lingeringly dwelt on. This is Robert Service's description of Armand from his book *Lenin: A Biography*: 'She had high, well-defined cheekbones. Her nose was slightly curved and her nostrils were wonderfully flared; her upper lip was slightly protrusive. Her teeth were white and even. She had lustrous, dark eyebrows. And she had kept her figure after having her children'.[6] Maybe it was the years in exile, or coping with five children while working in the underground revolutionary movement, that kept her so trim.

One of the few women deemed interesting in her own right is Alexandra Kollontai. Conventional histories of the Bolshevik Party tend to focus on her flamboyant beauty and glamour, her powers of oratory and her interest in sexual freedom. Feminist histories describe her as a lone voice, battling single-handedly to force the recalcitrant Bolsheviks to take women workers seriously. It took a female socialist historian, Cathy Porter, to write a biography that situated Kollontai at the heart of the Russian Revolution.[7]

For a hundred years, historians have ignored the role that women played in the revolution, not as wives and lovers, but as militant activists and as political leaders. Yet female workers were at the forefront of campaigns against the First World War, against punitive price rises and appalling working conditions. Their struggles shaped the Bolshevik Party as female socialists broke the mould of revolutionary organisation to reach out to and organise women. The female Bolsheviks deserve to take their place alongside their male comrades. They helped to construct the revolutionary organisations of Russia. They helped to sustain those organisations through years of repression. They helped to convince working men and women of the need to oppose imperialist war and to take power into their own hands. Focusing on the women who left their homes and families and endured hardship, prison and exile can add something both to our understanding of how the Bolsheviks won power and return the oppressed to their rightful place at the centre of revolutionary politics.

2. Russians in Paris: 'To the barricades!'

The great revolutionary Rosa Luxemburg observed that before a revolution happens, it is perceived as impossible, but that after it happens it is seen as having been inevitable. Female workers and socialists helped to make the impossible become possible. Russians did not have an indigenous revolutionary tradition to draw on. They had to look to the writings of Karl Marx and Frederick Engels and to the great European revolutions for inspiration. The greatest uprising of the late nineteenth century was the Paris Commune. The Communards' heroism revealed new realities about how the ruling classes maintained their power and how women, as well as men, could be mobilised to oppose it. Through a network of activists which included women, the Commune was to have a deep effect on socialist politics in Russia where it awakened a generation of revolutionaries.

On 18 March 1871, a group of Parisian women stood between a regiment of soldiers and their cannons. The women were determined to keep hold of the cannons so they could defend their city from Prussian soldiers. The French government had surrendered to the Prussians after months of fighting and a catastrophic siege of Paris. The Parisians, however, were determined to fight on. In the early hours of the morning, milkmaids delivering milk from house to house spread the news that the soldiers were taking the cannons. When the women of Paris confronted General Lecomte, he ordered his soldiers to fire on them. The women appealed to them shouting, 'Will you fire on us?' They would not. Instead they fraternised with them and the General was executed. By noon most of the cannons were in the hands of the Parisians.

This incident sparked the Paris Commune. The Communards rose up to take control of their city, one of the greatest cities in the world, and held it for two months. In the process, they challenged the existing social order and drew inspiration from ideas which included socialism and women's rights. 'Across the city, insurgent women enacted, inspired, theorized and led the revolution.'[8] These insurgent women smashed existing preconceptions of the role of women and asserted their right to participate in the creation of a new society. Very importantly, Russian women not only played a key role in the Commune, they also took their experiences back to the revolutionary movement in Russia.

In Russia in the 1860s, a 'great wind of revolution was blowing over the young generation of the intelligentsia.'[9] This was reflected in the literature of the time, such as Nicolas Chernyshevsky's 1863 novel *What is to be done?*, which was hugely influential. Russian women from the educated middle classes were beginning to strain against their repressive, patriarchal society and seek an education denied to them by the Tsarist authorities. Sophie Krukovsky wrote, 'A sort of epidemic spread among children, and especially among girls; the desire to flee from the paternal house'.[10] Sophie escaped from her wealthy military family to Switzerland where she became a distinguished mathematician. Her sister Anna travelled with her to Geneva where she met and married a revolutionary, Victor Jaclard, and made friends with another Russian radical, Elisabeth Dmitrieff. Then Anna Jaclard headed for Paris where she worked as a book binder and became active in the First International: 'she simultaneously discovered the necessity for work and the workers' revolution'.[11]

During the Commune, Anna Jaclard helped to establish the Montmartre Vigilance Committee, which organised workshops and ambulances, campaigned for women's rights and sent women to speak at the influential political clubs. Hostile contemporaries described how screeching women with crying babies and red sashes dominated some of these clubs. When the Commune issued an appeal for aid, Anne Jaclard's Committee proclaimed, 'The women of Montmartre, inspired by the revolutionary spirit, wish to attest by their actions to their devotion to the Revolution'.[12] Jaclard also founded and wrote for a socialist newspaper and corresponded with Karl Marx.

Another influential Communard organisation was the Union of Women, established by Anna's Russian friend, Elisabeth Dmitrieff. Dmitrieff was the daughter of unmarried parents, a rich Russian Hussar officer and a young nurse. She came of age in radical circles in the 1860s and she too headed for Switzerland where she met Russian revolutionaries who sent her to London to meet Karl Marx. She spent three months in London, talking with Karl Marx and his daughters Laura, Jenny and Eleanor, and meeting other socialists. A brief reference to Elisabeth in a letter written by Marx's daughter Jenny to her future husband suggests what a dedicated revolutionary Elisabeth was and hints at how women often had to choose between political activism and sexual relationships. Elisabeth did not want her friend to turn away from her political commitments and opt for a conventional marriage instead. Jenny described about how Elisabeth would respond if she read Jenny's love letters. 'How disgusted, how disappointed she would be! She who had set her heart upon making of me a heroine, a second Madame Roland… do not forget that it is you who have deprived the world of a heroine'.[13]

Marx appointed Dmitrieff as his envoy to Paris in 1871. She was just 20 years old, but she proved to be a charismatic and effective revolutionary leader. She established the Union of Women in April 1871 to build support for the Commune among working women. The Union organised women from many different occupations, including hatters, seamstresses, book binders, cardboard makers and gold polishers. The Union was at the heart of the Commune's attempts to reform both working conditions and the nature of work itself through a new system of workshops. Dmitrieff reported, 'In taking work away from the bondage of capitalistic exploitation, the formation of these organisations would eventually allow the workers to run their own businesses'.[14] Dmitrieff and Jaclard both fought for unity between male and female workers, opposing calls from men to exclude women from paid jobs so that they could not be used to undercut the higher wage rates paid to men.

When the French government launched its murderous assault on the Commune, Dmitrieff and many other women stayed on the barricades for days on end. Many thousands of Communards were shot dead, more were executed or transported. Anna Jaclard and her husband were captured. He was sentenced to death and she to hard labour for life. Fortunately, they managed to escape to London where they stayed with Karl Marx. On returning to Russia, Anna made contact with revolutionary groups around the People's Will, an organisation which advocated revolutionary violence to spur a peasants' revolt against the Tsar. Elisabeth Dmitrieff also escaped the repression and made her way back to Russia.

The experiences of the Paris Commune shaped the socialist tradition in Europe through the First International in particular, and both Jaclard and Dmitrieff were active in the Russian section. After the Commune, many socialists realised that working women could and should be won to the socialist cause. The experience of the Commune was the basis of a key section of Lenin's *State and Revolution*[15] and it laid the foundation of the Bolsheviks' understanding of the state. It stood as a terrible warning to those who thought they could rise up against their rulers without confronting the state and, as such, it was one of the many tributaries which flowed into the Russian Revolution.

3. The first revolutionaries: 'To the people!'

At the beginning of the twentieth century, the Russian Empire covered one sixth of the surface of the earth. It ruled over 150 million people made up of 170 different nationalities. Some twenty million peasants had only been freed from serfdom – personal bondage – in 1861. The Romanov dynasty had ruled Russia for 300 years and remained absolutist at heart. The extremely repressive nature of nineteenth-century Russian society bred extreme responses. In the years following the Paris Commune, a generation of young people agonised about how to address Russia's desperate inequalities. The 'To the People Movement' and 'Land and Liberty' sought to rouse the peasants to rebellion by educating them. However, women were themselves excluded from higher education in Russia. The first generation of Russian female revolutionaries sought to educate themselves, often at universities outside Russia, and in order to be able to educate the peasants. Some dressed as men as they tramped around villages with revolutionary pamphlets while others established egalitarian communes. When the peasantry failed to respond, a new organisation, 'People's Will' emerged. Its activists tried to precipitate a revolution by acts of violence and terrorism. Women were at the forefront of all these developments.

There was a sense among the young people that history was moving too slowly and that progress needed to be speeded up by gestures of self-sacrifice and martyrdom. The Tsarist regime was rotting from within and its barbarity was revealed in its response to this opposition. It launched a wave of repression against the student revolutionaries which culminated in October 1877, when thousands of young Russians were rounded up and arrested. The subsequent 'Trial of the 193' became the focal point of a multitude of grievances and served to fuel the movement. Among the few acquitted at this early trial was Sophia Perovskaya. Sophia had left her aristocratic family to become a terrorist revolutionary. She took part in four further attempts to assassinate Tsar Alexander II, finally succeeding on 1 March 1881. Aged only 27, she became the first woman to be executed for terrorism in Russia. Her courage and principled stand against tyranny made her a heroine to many women, including a young Alexandra Kollontai.[16]

Vera Figner was one of the few active revolutionaries to escape the crackdown in 1877. Like Sophia, she was born into a noble family, which she left to study medicine in Bern. She abandoned her studies to return home in order to revive the revolutionary cause. She became a leading member of the People's Will organisation, the same group with which Anna Jaclard had been associated. Like Sophia Perovskaya, Figner took part in the assassination of Alexander II and was arrested. She spent twenty months in solitary confinement and was then sentenced to death. Unlike Sophia Perovskaya, Figner's sentence was commuted and she spent twenty years in prison. In 1906, Figner was allowed to travel abroad where she campaigned for political prisoners and published a widely read pamphlet on Russian prisons. After the February Revolution of 1917 she was treated as an icon of the radical movement and when her memoirs were published after the 1917 Revolution they became a sensation in Russia and were translated into many other languages. Figner continued to work on behalf of prisoners for the rest of her life. 'The idea of martyrdom was instilled in girls by the Christian tradition,' Figner wrote, 'and was reinforced by the struggle for the rights of the oppressed.'[17]

Before her arrest, Vera Figner had been a political associate of another Vera – Vera Zasulich. Vera Zasulich was unusual in these circles because she was from a poor family and worked as a clerk in St Petersburg. She became involved with revolutionaries when she taught literacy to factory workers and she was imprisoned for four years in 1869. Following the 'Trial of the 193', she decided to assassinate Colonel Trepov in revenge for his mistreatment of prisoners. She succeeded in seriously wounding him. Her trial caused a sensation when Colonel Trepov's cruelty was exposed, and despite all the evidence Zasulich was acquitted by a jury. She fled to Switzerland and there became a committed Marxist and founding member of the Emancipation of Labour Group, which developed into the RSDLP. She helped to launch the socialist paper *Iskra* alongside Lenin and other leading Marxists. Zasulich was totally devoted to the revolutionary cause, although later her support for the Mensheviks against the Bolsheviks led her to oppose the October Revolution in 1917. Despite this, Trotsky retained his respect for Zasulich. He wrote after her death that she had combined both theoretical elements of Marxism and the 'moral political foundations' of the Russian radicals from the 1870s.[18] Zasulich and the opposition to Tsarism drew sympathy internationally. Oscar Wilde's first play, *Vera; or, The Nihilists*, was loosely based on her life.[19]

The 'moral foundations' of the Russian radicals of both sexes established a tradition of dedication and self-sacrifice. These early radicals demonstrated through example that women could play leading roles in the fight against tyranny. Their tradition was continued and developed by women growing up in the 1880s and 1890s who dedicated their lives to the cause of socialist revolution. Vera Zasulich was among a small number of courageous women who found their way from terrorism and radical populism to revolutionary politics. These women helped to construct a 'ramshackle bridge' for those who came after them.[20]

The women who joined the RSDLP, the organisation of revolutionary socialists, continued with the same idealism and self-sacrifice as the terrorists, but their courage was deployed not in assassinations but in working in the underground. They were famous for their *tverdost*, their unflinching dedication to the cause and their courage in facing down both Tsarist repression and the sexism of their own comrades. The generation of populists who sought to rouse the peasantry had demonstrated that courage was not enough. To challenge the Tsarist autocracy, with its spies, secret police, torture chambers and prison camps, they needed a more powerful social force. This they found at study circles, where they read Marx and Engels, and among the workers employed in Moscow and St Petersburg's huge factories, whom they taught at Sunday schools: it was the working class. The first Marxist revolutionaries smuggled letters and literature and established networks, risking imprisonment and exile to create revolutionary organisation in the heart of one of the most tyrannical regimes on earth.

At the turn of the twentieth century, the radical movement in Russia had revived after being crushed by the repression of the 1880s. These years saw many of the most influential revolutionary women join the RSDLP. So many made the difficult choice to become revolutionaries at the end of the nineteenth century that, by the turn of the twentieth century, Russia had more female radicals than any other nation in Europe.[21] They gave up their personal lives, lived without homes under the constant threat of arrest, imprisonment and exile. In the underground, women and men were treated equally; both sexes went without food, slept on floors, smuggled documents and lived with insecurity and fear. This first generation of female social democrats tended to be from the aristocracy or upper middle classes. That, however, was about to change.

4. 1905: 'A festival of the oppressed'

On 9 January 1905, a march of some 200,000 people tramped through the deep snow of St Petersburg's streets to present a petition to the Tsar. Their petition described how they were no long treated as human beings, but 'as slaves who must suffer their bitter fate in silence'.[22] The demonstrators were dressed in their Sunday best and carried pictures of the Tsar and religious icons. In fact, their faith in the Tsar had an almost religious fervour.

The Tsar had already left St Petersburg, but not before having deployed 12,000 troops to stop the petitioners from getting anywhere near his Winter Palace. On their way to the palace the marchers were confronted by a squadron of those troops. The soldiers lowered their rifles and fired into the crowd. People fell screaming to the ground but the soldiers kept firing. Blood stained the snow as hundreds of men, women and children were shot down. The massacre sparked a huge wave of strikes and protests right across the Russian Empire. The 1905 Revolution had begun. Alexandra Kollontai, who was to become one of the most prominent Russian revolutionaries, marched on the day that was to become known as Bloody Sunday. She described how the Tsar had unknowingly killed not only the demonstrators but also 'the workers' faith that they could ever achieve justice from him. From then on everything was different and new'.[23]

The revolution took many by surprise, but those connected with working women would have been familiar with their growing resistance to the hardships they endured. The 1904 war with Japan brought terrible conditions to the countryside and thousands of peasant women rebelled in what were sneeringly known as 'Babi Bunty': peasant women's riots. Many desperate women left their 'passivity and ignorance behind them', Alexandra Kollontai noted, and headed to the cities.[24] In 1904, a rising wave of industrial unrest swept across Russia, involving increasing numbers of women workers, especially in the textile industry. Some of the female members of the Bolshevik faction inside the RSDLP realised that their party could not lead the strike movement if they ignored the women.

However, the idea of appealing to women was controversial with many socialists and trade unionists, because women were overwhelmingly concentrated in unskilled, poorly organised industries and therefore appeared to lack the capacity to organise themselves. Female workers were also considered to be the most politically-backward section of the working class and were deemed to be a drag on the workers' movement. Alexandra Kollontai wanted to reach out to female workers but she too was frustrated by the conservatism of the women she met: 'The working women were still avoiding life and struggle, believing that their destiny was the cooking pot, the washtub and the cradle'.[25]

In the villages women expected their lives to be like those of their mothers, grandmothers and great-grandmothers, but poverty forced them into the cities and into the workplaces. Their insecurity meant that they tended to cling to the family structure, but the breakdown of their traditional ways of life also meant that they could be open to new ways of seeing the world. During the huge strike waves of 1905, female workers confounded expectations and began to organise. Laundry workers and domestic workers, who were overwhelmingly women, struck and tried to form trade unions: 'Women threw off the old servility, left their machines and gave the strike movement an unprecedented sense of solidarity and confidence'.[26]

In 1905 the Bolshevik Party was weak on the ground in Russia after years of arrests and repression. However, they did have a core of experienced members, which meant that

they could try to have an impact on events. Female Bolsheviks, for example, were very effective at smuggling weapons
from Finland into Russia. They could wear perfume to disguise the smell of dynamite and hide rifles in their skirts.
One particularly fearless courier, Feodosiya Drabkina, went
on missions across St Petersburg, taking her three-year old
daughter Lizka with her as cover. Lizka remembered being
puzzled at the way her mother would constantly change
shape, growing and shrinking as she carried and delivered
smuggled arms. The pair managed to smuggle bombs into
Moscow in December 1905 to aid the insurrection that had
been launched there.[27]

Women like Feodosiya were very courageous, but in
1905 the centre of the revolution was shifting away from
arms and street barricades and towards the workplaces and
the St Petersburg Soviet, an organ of direct working-class
democracy. Krupskaya, Lenin's wife, was one of many revolutionaries who were able to return home from exile in 1905.
She became secretary to the Bolshevik Central Committee,
where she experienced a sense of empowerment: 'It is difficult to imagine how we ever managed to cope with it all, and
how we kept things in order, being controlled by nobody,
and living "of our own free will".[28]

These professional female revolutionaries could win
respect from male workers. For example, Alexandra Kollontai was delegated to attend the first meeting of the St
Petersburg Soviet. Experienced female agitators like Kollontai, Krupskaya and Elena Stasova could also win newly
radicalised female workers to revolutionary socialism. The
Bolsheviks also had a small number of female members
inside the workplaces. Vera Karelina organised thousands
of women workers in support of the St Petersburg Assembly
of Factory and Mill operatives in 1904. This assembly organised the strike in the Putilov Works and their demonstration
in January 1905 was one of the catalysts of the revolution.
On 3 June 1905, 11,000 women textile workers came out on
strike near Moscow, in one of the largest strikes ever seen in

Russia. Some 28 women were shot dead and Olga Gankina, a Bolshevik activist, was brutally murdered by Black Hundreds thugs when she was discovered with a suitcase full of weapons. Her example inspired other women to join the street fighting groups. Even after the revolution had been defeated, in 1907, these textile workers had the confidence to strike to win a half day off every week to do the laundry.

The RSDLP swelled by thousands during the revolution. The new members had more experience of direct struggle than those who had survived in the underground movement. Women politicised by the events of 1905 joined the Bolshevik Party not in women's usual roles as couriers and secretaries but as nurses, street fighters and agitators. The 1905 Revolution bequeathed to the Bolshevik Party a network of committed female activists inside some of St Petersburg's huge factories, and a core of female leaders determined to reach out to women and win them to socialism with new organisations and publications. The revolution revealed how the most backward and downtrodden workers could be transformed by events and be at the forefront of revolutionary struggle.

The actions of these women workers showed that they did not need to spend years in trade unions or socialist organisations to prepare themselves for revolution. Even women who had recently arrived in the big cities from the stultifying world of the villages could quickly learn how to organise, how to fight and what sort of changes they wanted to fight for. Reflecting on the experience of the 1905 Revolution, Lenin wrote: 'Revolutions are the festival of the oppressed and the exploited. At no other time are the masses of the people in a position to come forward so actively as creators of a new social order as at time of revolution. At such times, the people are capable of performing miracles.'[29]

5. Terror, suffrage and socialism

The 1905 Revolution was suppressed and thousands were killed. January 1906 was known as the 'month of the firing squads'.[30] There were various responses to the experiences of revolution and counterrevolution. Some women turned in frustration back to terrorism, a tradition which continued to run deep in Russian revolutionary politics. Maria Spiridonova was first arrested during the student demonstrations of March 1905. In September 1905, she joined the Socialist-Revolutionary Party (SR), and became a full-time activist. Like many SRs, she embraced the idea of assassination and terrorism as a revolutionary weapon. Spiridonova's target was GN Luzhenovsky, a landowner and councillor notorious for the brutal suppression of peasant unrest. Spiridonova volunteered to kill him and shot him down on 16 January 1906. He died on 10 February.

Spiridonova was immediately captured by Luzhenovsky's Kossack body guards. A few days later a newspaper published a letter from her, in which she described the abuse and torture she had suffered following her arrest. She had been stripped, whipped, burnt, beaten and sexually assaulted. Her experience caused widespread outrage among liberal opinion. On 11 March, Spiridonova was tried and convicted of Luzhenovsky's murder and sentenced to death. However, the sentence was commuted to penal servitude in Siberia where she spent 11 terrible years. After the February Revolution of 1917, she was released under an amnesty for political prisoners. She led the left-wing faction of the Socialist Revolutionaries in supporting the October Revolution, although she later fell out with the Soviet government.

Other women looked to new constitutional possibilities. By October 1905 the Tsar had been forced to concede a

Duma – a parliament – or more accurately, a dress-rehearsal for a parliament, but women were excluded from it. Before the Duma was set up, men and women had a form of political equality: neither had any democratic rights. Now, with limited male suffrage, campaigns for women's suffrage familiar in the West began to develop in Russia. A vigorous and effective feminist movement emerged which expressed both women's new-found political activism and their frustration. The Russian feminist movement had largely consisted of philanthropy and campaigning for access to education for girls. Now feminists were campaigning for political rights for women, and their campaign sought to bring together women of all classes to win the vote. The Russian Women's League, for example, explicitly sought to unite 'ladies and their maids' to campaign together to win the right to vote in Duma elections.

An All Russian Women's Congress was organised in St Petersburg in December 1908 to animate and unify the women's movement. The Social Democrats remained hostile to participation in such a feminist gathering. The socialists argued that working-class women had more in common with the men of their class than with the ladies who employed them. They wanted men and women to fight for expanded suffrage and for increased democracy. Kollontai sought to challenge the feminists by proposing socialist solutions to women's problems, based on increased wages, maternity leave and protective legislation. After initial reluctance, the St Petersburg socialists sanctioned a delegation. Armand and Kollontai both participated in the Congress.

Alexandra Kollontai realised that there was a contest between feminism and socialism for the allegiance of the politicised women workers. Feminist movements across Europe sought to unite all women, regardless of social class, to fight for their political rights against their enemy – men. In practise, the bourgeois feminist often had little understanding of, or will to address, the problems faced by working women. Kollontai pioneered a tactic of heckling feminists at meetings to put forward demands that would improve life for working women. In the weeks before the All-Russian Women's Congress in December 1908, Kollontai organised a group of working women to put their case for social reforms. The women identified themselves by wearing red carnations on their cheap dresses. The well-to-do women seated on the platform hissed and stamped their feet as Kollontai's labour group put forward their demands. Provoked, one shouted out, 'What do you know of our lives, bowling along in your carriages while we get splashed with mud?'[31] It was a pithy description of the gulf opening up between the socialists and the bourgeois feminists.

Kollontai also campaigned for the recognition of women's demands at factory meetings and working men's clubs. By spring 1906, Kollontai and some of her friends had established discussion groups for women workers, based on the very limited socialist publications aimed at women – Krupskaya's pamphlet, *The Woman Worker* (1900), and a new pamphlet, *The Woman's Lot* (1905). They argued that women's oppression was rooted in the privatised family and the exploitation inherent in capitalism, drawing on the writings of Frederick Engels and August Bebel.

Kollontai's audacity and innovative tactics, combined with her political depth, proved successful in recruiting female workers. One such recruit was Alexandra Artiukhina. She grew up without a father and in 1903 her mother was sacked and blacklisted for striking. The family moved to St Petersburg where an uncle was a revolutionary activist. Both women found work and Alexandra became a leader in the textile workers' union and joined the Bolsheviks in 1910. Artiukhina later recalled how important the women's clubs were to the process of recruitment. In the clubs, women were brought to a realisation of their human dignity and became acquainted with the names of women like Sofia Perovskaya and Vera Figner: 'We read the works of Marx, Engels and Lenin. We understood that the enslavement of women occurred together with the establishment of private ownership of the means of production and the beginning of exploitation of man by man and that real equality and real freedom for women would be found only in socialism, where there would be no exploitation of man by man.'[32]

As the revolutionary tide of 1905 ebbed, revolutionaries were forced back into exile. In September 1906, Kollontai travelled to Finland where she met up with Lenin and Krupskaya and with Rosa Luxemburg, who was writing her famous account of the mass strike movement. Kollontai returned to Germany with Rosa Luxemburg to attend an international conference of socialists in Stuttgart where she met the Marxist and campaigner for women's rights, Clara Zetkin. These three leading revolutionary women would have had many theoretical and practical insights to share with each other. In August 1907, Alexandra joined Clara Zetkin at the Stuttgart Socialist Women's Conference, the first socialist conference devoted to women's issues. Another Conference of Socialist Women was held in Copenhagen in 1910.

These discussions were dominated by issues such as the women's campaign for suffrage. The European socialist parties 'before the First World War were virtually alone in the political world in including an explicit demand for female suffrage in their programmes.'[33] However, support for women's suffrage could be based on the belief that women's role as mothers and wives meant that they could purify public life. Attitudes to female suffrage differentiated socialists, who tended to support universal suffrage, from feminists, who more often supported votes for women on the same restricted basis as existing male suffrage. Debates around suffrage also led to discussions around the limitations of formal political equality and women's role at work and in the family.

It was at such gatherings that socialist women began to theorise a new political reality which had been revealed in 1905: the rise of female workers. In the great industrial cities of Moscow and St Petersburg there had been a significant growth in the number of female workers. Between 1901 and 1914 the Russian labour force grew by 37 percent. Some 65 percent of the new workforce were women. In some industries, such as textiles, women made up over 50 percent of the workforce. However, the ideas that dominated the workers' movement had not yet recognised the new reality. Female workers were still considered particularly backward by many trade unionists and some socialists. In 1912 women made up just six percent of trade union membership. An article in the Bolshevik paper *Pravda* explained that this low rate of union membership reflected women's backwardness and their role in undercutting men's wages. Women were more likely to be unskilled and illiterate and had to cope with the demands of domestic labour as well as paid employment. Few male workers supported the idea of equal pay for equal work.

Bolshevik organisation had always promoted the idea of women's equality within the movement. In the hard years of the underground movement there was little other choice. However, many male socialists felt that women should wait for the revolution to deliver their liberation, and to raise any demands before that was to risk dividing the movement. Many working-class women were not prepared to accept the conditions forced on them and looked to the trade unions and socialists for support. The pressures on female workers compelled them to organise and seek to defend themselves through working-class organisations. This meant challenging the prejudice and hostility of male workers and forcing reluctant socialists to hear and listen to them.

Hundreds of working women wrote to *Pravda* to give voice to their complaints about poor working conditions and lack of male solidarity. Their letters convinced female Bolsheviks including Armand, Krupskaya, Samoilova, and Zinovieva to argue for a new strategy of reaching out to women workers with a special magazine. The success of the resultant Women's Day in 1913 supported their argument.

These women were not the stereotypes of passive, ignorant Babas (a derogatory word for peasant women). In February 1914, *Pravda* devoted several pages to articles about women and a meeting followed. Anna Ulyanova, Lenin's older sister, described the meetings as, 'the first major action by working women which played an immense, decisive role in the women workers' movement'.[34] The militancy of working women encouraged the Bolshevik women, and the strategy adopted by the socialist women encouraged female militancy. The Bolshevik women understood how many women were propelled by their experience of exploitation to seek collective solutions. This process would be accelerated by the turmoil created by the First World War.

An artist's impression of Lenin on the sealed train. Note the lack of women!

Elisabeth Dmitrieff

The execution of Sophia Perovskaya.

Vera Figner

Delegates to the Stuttgart Congress in 1907. Spot the women!

Demonstration on Nevsky Prospekt after the February Revolution.

An issue of *Rabotnitsa* (Woman Worker).

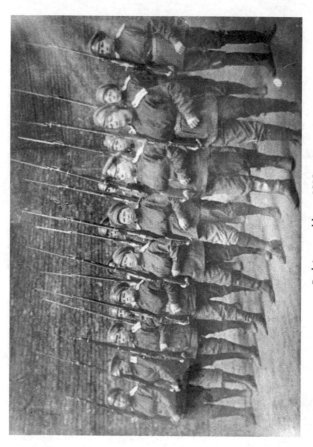

Red Army soldiers, 1918.

A traditional peasant family in Russia, c.1917.

Alexander Rodchenko's powerful advertisement for a bookshop.

6. 1914: The disasters of war

The outbreak of the First World War prompted a wave of nationalism across Europe. The mighty socialist parties of the Marxist Second International had proudly committed themselves to opposing war by any means. Faced with real war, however, they collapsed into supporting the war effort of their own ruling classes while offering left-wing-sounding justifications for their capitulation. Revolutionaries who stayed true to their principled opposition to imperialism and war were devastated, Lenin even allowing himself the temporary luxury of disbelieving newspaper reports of the capitulation. These socialists were initially isolated, persecuted and abused, but as the war dragged on, killing millions of young men in the trenches and causing severe poverty and hardship at home, the mood across the working classes of Europe began to shift. The socialists who had stood firm thus found themselves in a position to lead this growing opposition to the bloodshed.

Middle-class feminists and suffrage campaigners in country after country fell in behind their own national armies. Emmeline Pankhurst was in Russia in 1917 drumming up support for the allied war effort. However, the leading figures of the Socialist Women's International all remained true to their opposition to imperialist war, in stark contrast to the male leaders of the parent body, the Second International. 'Louise Saumoneau in France, Alexandra Kollontai, Nadezhda Krupskaya and Inessa Armand in Russia (or in the exiled leadership of the Russian socialists in Zurich), Clara Zetkin and Luis Zietz in Germany, all opposed the war from the start.'[35]

The socialist women organised the Bern Conference in March 1915. With some 70 delegates, this conference was a crucial step towards building opposition to the war. The

Bolshevik delegation, led by Krupskaya, argued that the socialist parties should break away from their patriotic comrades and work to overthrow their own ruling classes. Thus, from the outbreak of war the Bolsheviks' courageous and principled stand against imperialism was at the core of their theory and their practice. It would prove decisive in the years ahead, as tens of thousands of people were driven by bitter experience to oppose the war.

The First World War had brought about huge changes in the lives of women. The majority of Russian women lived in villages where life was unendurably hard. Article 107 of the Imperial Code of Civil Laws stated that, 'a wife must obey her husband as the head of the family, live with him in love, treat him with esteem, utmost respect, obedience and humility due to him as master of the house.' Women needed their husband's permission to travel or work. There was no contraception and women endured multiple pregnancies. Infant mortality rates were high and infanticide was not uncommon. Women's survival strategies were based on passivity and fatalism. These expectations and attitudes were brutally uprooted by the outbreak of war.

Men were conscripted to the front and women began to replace them in the factories and workplaces. Large numbers of women had already found jobs in Russia's towns and cities, but the process accelerated dramatically after 1914 when some 40 percent of industrial workers left for the front. In 1914 only three percent of workers in the metal industry were women; by 1917 it was 18 percent. Around one quarter of industrial workers were women in 1914; by 1917 it was nearly half. Women were usually, but not exclusively, concentrated in unskilled jobs. In the factories, women endured terrible hardships with no legal protection. Women discovered to be pregnant were sacked on the spot and were often so desperate to cling to their jobs that they hid pregnancies. One worker remembered, 'The women workers used to hide it until their mouths foamed and the child was born at the bench... There used to be many women workers who cursed their children'.[36] Prostitution was also a way of life for many women in the cities. However, even as women endured these terrible hardships, the nature of work in the big industrial plants propelled them towards the traditions of collective organisation which had existed before the war.

The nineteenth century had seen industrialisation and the development of the Russian working class. From the late nineteenth century, strikes and labour organisations grew, and large-scale strikes in the textile industry involved many female workers. Mass strike movements were the engine of the 1905 Revolution and they developed political as well as economic demands. Strikes broke out in the years before the First World War; in 1912 one million workers took part in strike action. This militancy was disrupted by the outbreak of the war. By the beginning of 1917, the women were recreating the traditions of workplace militancy that had existed among the male industrial workers before the war. It took the women just months to rediscover the militant traditions that had been built over decades before the war.

As the war ground on, St Petersburg, now renamed Petrograd, suffered from terrible shortages in fuel and basic foodstuffs. Peasants had been conscripted into the army on a huge scale and this led to a fall in food production but the shortages were exacerbated by profiteering. The eight-hour working day was at that time an unachievable dream, so after their shifts, working women had to join the queues for bread. Ella Woodhouse, the daughter of the British consul in Petrograd, employed a maid whose only job was to stand in queues for milk and bread.[37] The queues were up to a mile long, with women standing four abreast. They could begin queueing before dawn in freezing temperatures, only to be told there would be no bread that day. Meanwhile, Petrograd's wealthy were dining on caviar, pâté de foie gras, venison, pheasant and champagne.[38] There were rumours of speculators stockpiling food and widespread government corruption. Women began chalking slogans on factory walls: 'Bring our men home', 'Give us bread.' They began organising as workers and as soldiers' wives.

In the first weeks of 1917, the Duma's response to the growing crisis was to ban the baking of cakes, buns, pies and biscuits and to restrict the supply of flour to workers' canteens. Workers greeted the bans with rage. Some observers were reassured that the growing anger was economic rather than political in nature, but the division between the two was dissolving as the war and the hardship dragged on. In workplaces and barracks, streets and markets, socialists were linking hunger to the war and to the autocratic government itself. Within a few weeks, the people were demanding more than cakes and buns. British ambassador George Buchanan believed that the coming storm would begin, 'not with the workmen in the factories, but with the crowds waiting in the cold and the snow outside the provision shops'.[39]

Sections of the Bolshevik party had begun to realise that female workers were not a drain on the movement, that they not were irrevocably conservative. They began to listen to soldiers' wives and women workers freezing in the endless queues for food. When they organised against the war, Bolshevik party members organised amongst the women. There were huge debates between party members about whether to have separate organisations which aimed to win women over to socialism. A publication directed at women was launched. *Rabotnitsa* (Woman Worker) grew out of the Bolshevik paper *Pravda* when a special women's issue was inundated with letters from women, expressing their grievances and demands.

Rabotnitsa was initially accepted by the censors. On the eve of publication, however, the police raided an editorial board meeting and arrested all the members except for Anna Ulyanova who arrived late for the meeting. Undeterred, she produced the first edition single handedly. It sold out of 12,000 copies but the paper was definitively shut down in June after seven issues. Although short-lived, the paper was influential. The links made and political support won among female factory workers in 1914 through *Rabotnitsa* were to stand the Bolsheviks in good stead in 1917. Such principled opposition to the war became especially important after the February Revolution when 'defencism', the idea of supporting Russia's war effort to defend the gains made by the Revolution, developed into a powerful current in the socialist movement. Kollontai and Lenin and their supporters opposed all justifications for continuing the war. The Bolsheviks' militant and consistent opposition to the war proved to be vital in winning working women to the socialist cause.

7. 'We Bolsheviks felt as though we had grown wings'[40]

Nicolai Sukharnov, a prominent socialist, was in Petrograd in February 1917. He overheard two female typists talking about the anger of the women queuing for bread in the snow. They concluded that a revolution was beginning. Sukharnov dismissed them as 'philistine girls'. 'Revolution – highly improbable! Revolution – everyone knew this was only a dream!'[41] Yet the 'girls' were right and the experienced revolutionary was wrong. On International Women's Day, the anger of the women queuing for food coalesced with the grievances of women in the factories and exploded onto the streets of St Petersburg. The women ignited the February Revolution and unleashed a huge social movement. Within a few weeks, the Tsar had been forced to abdicate in favour of the Provisional Government, which was to rule until elections could be organised. Meanwhile, tens of thousands of workers and soldiers created a movement capable of running society for themselves through their own democratic councils, or soviets.

The February Revolution is often portrayed as a spontaneous, leaderless revolution; a revolution started accidently by women who only cared about providing for their families. These women were just too emotional and ill-disciplined to listen to the seasoned socialists who advised patience and caution: their very courage is cited as evidence of their lack of political understanding. As Trotsky described it, those who opposed the revolution were keen to prove that it was merely, 'a petticoat rebellion, backed up afterwards by a soldiers' mutiny'[42] masquerading as a revolution. Historian after historian proclaimed that the masses moved by themselves, that there were no leaders, only threatening elements. The secret police noted that the February Revolution was not directed by leaders from above, but they also noted the 'generally propagandised condition of the proletariat'.[43]

That propaganda did not appear from thin air; it was written, published and distributed. Trotsky described how unnamed, unacknowledged leaders among the working classes nourished themselves on fragments of revolutionary propaganda and dissected the liberal press: 'In every factory, in each guild, in each company, in each tavern, in the military hospital, at the transfer stations, even in the depopulated villages, the molecular work of revolutionary thought was in progress'.[44] Politicised workers led the February Revolution and women were in the forefront both in the workplaces and in the Bolshevik Party. Focusing on the role of female Bolsheviks reveals how revolutionaries did help both to ignite the February Revolution and to sustain that revolution through to its victory in October. Women were part of the revolutionary process from the beginning and did not retreat into the background after the overthrow of the Tsar.

In February 1917, the working women of the militant Vyborg District of Petrograd were planning to mark International Women's Day with street protests and strikes. The Bolshevik Party, whose leadership was still largely in exile, advised caution. The party wanted the women to wait and to 'stir the masses to boiling point' for a general strike on May Day. International Women's Day had only been celebrated for two years and had always been a relatively small event in Russia. The Vyborg District of St Petersburg was home to many engineering plants and textile factories, and to a strong revolutionary tradition. The night before International Women's Day, a skilled metal worker and experienced Bolshevik, Kayurov, was sent to talk to the women. 'I endeavoured first and foremost to urge the women to refrain from any abortive deeds and to act only upon the instructions given by the party Committee', Kayurov recalled. The women told him they had run out of patience: their husbands were dying at the front and their children were hungry. The next day he learnt with 'astonishment' and 'indignation' that the women had ignored his advice and had gone out on strike.[45] They downed tools and faced down the men who told them that protest was 'not the business of Babas.' Some 900,000 workers joined them on strike on the first day.

This is the conventional view of the February Revolution: militant but unpolitical women stirred things up and forced a reluctant Bolshevik Party to back their strikes. The argument between Kayurov and the women is taken as proof that the women acted instinctively and without political strategy. 'If future historians look for the groups that began the Russian Revolution, let him not create any involved theory. The Russian Revolution was begun by hungry women and children demanding 'bread and herrings', diarist Pitirim Sorokin wrote.[46]

In fact, food was itself a deeply political issue. The Bolsheviks had long campaigned to channel anger over food shortages and high prices in a socialist direction. In 1915 the Bolsheviks published a pamphlet, *The War and the High Cost of Living*, which linked hunger, war and Tsarism. 'They drove our sons, brothers and husbands away to war, and deprived us of bread',[47] the pamphlet proclaimed. An official of the Petrograd District Court testified that the workers on the streets on 23 February were organised around slogans from the Bolsheviks' pamphlet. The pamphlet ended with a call for workers to take to the streets with the red banners of insurrection – exactly what they did in February 1917. The Bolshevik organisation in Russia was not a homogenous, centralised party. Some leaders inside Russia argued for caution, while party activists were fermenting revolt. The women had listened to the Bolsheviks' arguments and were prepared to act on them, even though party leaders thought the right moment had not yet come.

Women were prominent in the anti-war agitation in the Vyborg District. A network of female Bolsheviks in the area had organised a women's meeting which linked the economic issues of high prices and inflation with political opposition to the war. The St Petersburg Committee of the Bolshevik Party established a women's circle tasked with organisation and propaganda among the female factory workers. Leading members of the women's circle joined with women from the Bolshevik Interdistrict Committee to organise an event for International Women's Day. They planned to stage a joint anti-war demonstration which would again link the high cost of living with the war. They sent women speakers out to address workers' meetings and, while the Bolshevik Party failed to issue a leaflet for the day because its press had broken down, the women's Interdistrict Committee issued this appeal:

> *Dear women comrades, are we going to put up with this in silence much longer, now and then venting our smouldering rage on small shop owners? After all, they're not to blame for the people's suffering, they are being ruined themselves. The government is to blame! It started the war and cannot end it. The government is ruining the country and causing us to go hungry. The capitalists are to blame! The war brings them profits. It's high time to cry out to them: 'Enough!' Down with the criminal government and its whole gang of robbers and murderers! Long live peace!*[48]

A police official described what happened at the Aivaz Works. Over 3,000 female workers returned from their lunch break and gathered for a rally to celebrate Women's Day. 'The workers decided not to work today and began to talk about the bread crisis. The women asked the men to join them in a strike, and together they "peacefully dispersed'".[49] The peaceful dispersal meant that the workers left their factories, but they did not go home. In workplace after workplace, women struck and convinced men to join them, held impromptu demonstrations and rallies and clashed with the police. The Bolshevik Central Committee noted that it was, 'the insistence of the organised women' that sparked the uprising.[50]

The women working at the Neva Thread Mills heard a strange noise which became clearer as it got louder: It was voices outside shouting, 'Into the street! Stop! We've had it! And the entire first floor of the thread mill opened its windows in a flash, or rather they were knocked out with sticks, stones, and pieces of wood. The women thread-spinners surged noisily into the passageway... All the doors were thrown open. And the crowd of thread-makers pushed out into freedom'.[51] The women then went on to a metal works. A Bolshevik worker in the Ludwig Nobel Machinery Works recalled:

> *The morning of 23 February, women's voices were heard in the alley, shouting "Down with the War! Down with the high cost of living! Bread for the workers!" Myself and a few other comrades immediately went to the windows... The gates of the Boshoi Mill No1 were wide open. Throngs of militant women workers filled the alley. Those who spotted us began waving their arms and yelling "Come out, stop work!" Snowballs pelted the windows. We decided to join the demonstration.[52]*

The women linked arms with the men and, shouting hurrah, set off to the next mill. Some 30,000 workers from the Putilov Iron Works had been locked out days before. Now they were joined by striking workers and many spent hours in the streets, debating and marching.

The wealthy of Petrograd had their own defences to stop workers from districts like the Vyborg from penetrating their areas of the city: bridges that could be raised, rivers that could not be crossed and well-armed troops. All afternoon the workers gathered, were dispersed, and gathered again. Their aim was to reach the city's main square, the Nevsky Prospekt. Soldiers patrolled the trams, and they threw off anyone in workers' clothes. The next day, however, the Kossacks' discipline began to break down. When mounted soldiers were sent against the women protesters, the women encircled them and began to argue with them. A Bolshevik woman working in the Promet Factory, Alexandra Kruglova, recalled one confrontation:

> A detachment of Cossacks bore down on us quickly. But we did not waver and we stood in a solid wall as though turned to stone. An officer of Cossacks yelled, "Who are you following: You are being led by an old crone!" I said, "No old crone, but a sister and wife of soldiers at the front". What happened next was totally unexpected. The soldiers of the Novocherkassk Regiment lowered their rifles... Someone at the rear yelled, "Cossacks, you are our brothers, you can't shoot us". And the Cossacks turned their horses round.[53]

The Kossacks guarding the St Petersburg's main bridges put their sabres down. Workers swarmed across frozen river banks and Petrograd's leafy squares were occupied by workers waving red flags. Between speeches the crowds sung the *Marseillaise*, which the Tsar's government had deemed to be treasonous.

Zhenia Egorova, the secretary of the Vyborg District Bolshevik Party, also led the women in trying to separate the soldiers from their officers. Bolshevik Party members Nina Agadzhanova and Mariia Vydrina organised mass meetings, strikes, demonstrations and searches for hidden weapons they could use to arm the crowd. The women who were not considered capable of organising themselves or of developing political consciousness had brought the industry and services of St Petersburg to a standstill and pushed the garrison towards mutiny.

The beliefs that had held for centuries were blown away in days. People woke up praying for the health of the imperial family and ended the day shouting 'Down with the Tsar!'. There was an unprecedented reversal of rank and status in the most despotic, hierarchical society in Europe. An American journalist recalled, 'I found the capital delirious with freedom, the people still blinking in the light of the sudden deliverance'.[54] Before the war, the only job women were allowed to perform on St Petersburg's tram network was cleaning. A young, working-class woman called Alexandra Rodionova was one of the first to operate a tram. In 1916, she took part in her first strike and joined the Bolshevik Party. On International Women's Day 1917, Rodionova noticed that armed soldiers were guarding the tram depots, but by the end of the day they had joined the strikers. The women overturned trams to act as barricades in order to stop more troops being sent to crush them. Like many others, Rodionova experienced intense euphoria after the February Revolution. She remembered, 'It seemed to me that I had lost touch with solid ground and flew in giddy uncertainty. And suddenly, all at once, the unknown future became real'.[55] After the repression of the July days when leading Bolsheviks were forced into hiding, Rodionova hid 42 rifles in her depot. In October, she ensured that two trams left her depot to take weapons for the storming of the Winter Palace. She kept trams running throughout the October Revolution to help the revolutionaries to take power.

Women had to throw off centuries of oppression to claim their place in the revolution. They had to face down Kossacks armed with whips, the ingrained sexism and prejudice of male workers, and their own lack of confidence and experience. The fact that some women achieved this is testimony to the potential of self-emancipation of the working class to win women's liberation. However, the women and men who overthrew Tsarism in February 1917 could draw on a set of political ideas that linked their hunger to the war and to the whole autocratic political system. The Bolshevik Party argued, fought and agitated for socialist politics and it was the Bolsheviks who provided some of the most inspirational and courageous leaders for the 'leaderless' revolt.

8. February to October: 'We will not be handed our rights on a plate'[56]

On 21 April 1917 a crowd of female textile workers demonstrated against the Provisional Government, demanding bread and an end to the war. The female strikers were jeered by government supporters on the other side of the street: 'Stockingless! Uneducated riff raff! Ignoble sluts!' A striker retorted, 'You lot are wearing hats made by our hands!' A fight broke out and hat pins were used as weapons.[57] This small incident dramatises the failure of the Provisional Government to deliver what the working women were demanding: bread and peace. Throughout the summer, support was slipping away from the Provisional Government in the direction of the soviets, and away from the moderate socialists towards the revolutionaries.

The masses of Petrograd and Moscow were revelling in their new-found freedoms to meet, debate and organise. However, Kollontai was right when she declared that women would not get their rights handed to them on a plate. The Provisional Government dragged its heels over giving women the right to vote. Many men, especially in the villages, opposed female suffrage because they feared that voting might give women the confidence to resist being treated like beasts of burden. One report to the Duma recorded a peasant man saying, 'You stir up our women, and then they will not go into the shafts.'[58] Some men on the left argued that women were too reactionary and conservative to be allowed the vote.

Alexandra Kollontai returned from exile to Russia in March and immediately threw herself into the campaign for universal suffrage. 'But wasn't it we women, with our grumbling about hunger, about the disorganisation in Russian life, about our poverty and the sufferings born of the war, who awakened a popular wrath? And didn't we women go first out to the streets in order to struggle with our brothers for freedom, and even if necessary to die for it?'[59] After a 40,000-strong protest march, the government eventually granted universal women's suffrage in July 1917. Women over the age of 30 were granted the right to vote in England the following year. English women did not win universal suffrage until 1928.

Following the February Revolution, increasing numbers of women were no longer prepared to stand in line and wait for reforms to be handed to them. They began to take matters into their own hands. Workers in the huge factories of Petrograd have long been recognised as the motor of the revolution. However, the strength of the movement meant that previously unorganised workers were also drawn into the struggle, finding the confidence to demand both respect and better working conditions.

In Petrograd, a British resident noticed that his two maidservants would 'spend hours standing at street corners along the Nevsky Prospekt listening to orators preaching about equality and justice. After one such outing, they returned and told him and his wife that they were in future going to the cinema every night and intended to work no more than eight hours a day'.[60] Some maids and servants demanded their rights collectively and went on strike. The Bolshevik Party's paper, *Pravda*, reported how their meeting overflowed onto the streets. 'Comrade maids!' a woman wrote, 'We need a bigger hall!' Waitresses formed a union and used *Pravda* to appeal for support from 'all women comrades working in the tea rooms of Petrograd'.[61]

Some Bolshevik women saw the huge potential in these strikes and wanted to develop new ways to build support amongst the women. Not everyone in the Bolshevik Party agreed with them. Many leading socialist men and women believed that organising women separately from men represented a feminist threat to working-class unity. Kollontai proposed a Women's Bureau to organise women around their newly-won right to vote in elections. She was defeated at the Petrograd Party Conference in April 1917. Krupskaya described how hostility from male comrades discouraged her when she was trying to organise meetings of emigrant women milliners and dressmakers. Men would come to the meetings to heckle and dispute the need for separate women's meetings.[62] Nor did all the female workers embrace the revolution. When Kollontai found that the most downtrodden women could be the most conservative she sought Lenin's advice: 'Don't worry if the most downtrodden are the most reactionary', he told her. 'Their lives will be the hardest and they will be the first to understand what the Bolsheviks want.'[63] Under pressure from women's growing militancy, the party became increasingly sympathetic to the idea of making special efforts to organise working women and soldiers' wives. It was a strategy that won vital support for the Bolshevik Party.

On 1 May 1917, a strike of some 4,000 laundresses began in Petrograd. The women were particularly despised and downtrodden, toiling for 14 hours a day, paid a pittance and enduring health conditions such as rheumatism. They demanded an eight-hour day and refused the Provisional Government's instruction to return to work, choosing instead to tour the city's laundries extinguishing the fires used to heat the water. One of the strike leaders was a Bolshevik, Anna Sakharova. She invited Alexandra Kollontai to speak to the strikers and Kollontai encouraged the Bolsheviks to recognise the political significance of the strike by publishing a series of articles in *Pravda*.

Kollontai spent every day with the laundresses, persuading them to add Bolshevik slogans against the war to their demands for a shorter day. *Pravda* carried regular updates, appeals for financial support and lists of the names of strike breakers. Bolshevik members Ekaterina Shalaginova and Iadviga Netupskaya organised laundresses' unions in their neighbourhoods, while Kollontai organised a city-wide union. The laundresses stayed out on strike for a month before the employers gave in. Kollontai wrote a *Pravda* article called, 'In the Front Line of Fire', arguing that the women could no longer be called the 'backward and unaware section of the people'.[64] The laundresses had demonstrated that formerly unorganised and unskilled workers could take collective action and defeat their bosses. The laundresses' militancy revealed both workers' growing frustration with the Provisional Government and the political development of women workers.

Another group of women who played a key role in the events of 1917 were the soldiers' wives. Widespread hatred of the war was a key factor in the revolution. By 1917, some 15 million Russians were serving in the army, 1.8 million had been killed, four million wounded and three million were prisoners of war. The Provisional Government failed to end the war and instead launched the June Offensive in the name of the revolution. It was a disaster. The Bolsheviks emerged as the only party calling for an immediate end to the war.

The soldiers' wives have been excluded from most mainstream accounts of 1917. They were dismissed by contemporaries as 'blind moles', capable of nothing more than pleading with the authorities for help. The sympathy offered in the democratic press to these 'poor, illiterate women' implied or stated directly that the women lacked political ideas and acted only out of base instinct. They were portrayed as depoliticised, the objects of charity and pity. Male politicians and journalists refused to recognise the soldiers' wives as a political force in their own right.[65] When the women did express revolutionary aspirations it was taken as further evidence of their 'dark consciousness'.[66]

The soldiers' wives were a hugely diverse group of women but they were united by common grievances such as low allowances, the rising cost of food and fuel and high taxes. The soldiers' wives formed local unions. Some soviets initiated such unions and invited them to send delegates, whereas other unions were initiated by the women themselves. Some of the soldiers' wives' unions were led by women. The soldiers' wives learned how to organise collective action and they often won their demands. In the process, they threw off their traditional subservience and became increasingly militant in outlook. During the summer of 1917, a significant number moved away from supporting moderate socialists and embraced Bolshevism, mirroring the political developments taking place in the wider working class.[67]

The mass conscription of Russian men meant that by 1917 there were around 36 million Russians claiming state support. From 1912, soldiers' wives were able to claim a government allowance, but women who were not married in the eyes of the Orthodox Church were excluded. The Provisional Government ended this discrimination and granted allowances to soldiers' common-law wives and step-children, but they failed to raise the allowance. When the women responded to the failures of the Provisional Government there was an ideological contest for their allegiance and once again, it was the feminists versus Alexandra Kollontai. The feminists organised protests in which they encouraged the soldiers' wives to carry pro-war placards. In response, Kollontai took the initiative to organise her own demonstration. On 11 April, some 15,000 soldiers' wives marched on the Petrograd Soviet demanding a raise in their allowances and an end to the war.

The period from the February Revolution to October saw the Provisional Government and the soviets compete for authority. During these months, the Provisional Government saw its power ebb away towards the soviets, which were based on workplace democracy rather than parliament. It is, therefore, significant that while the Provisional Government was the formal legislature, the women marched to the soviet. They sensed where the power in society was beginning to reside. The chairman of the soviet, a Menshevik called Dan, came out to tell the women, 'Seek not more money but an end to the war'. 'That's rich, coming from a Menshevik!' Kollontai heckled.[68] When she was refused the right to address the women, Kollontai organised an impromptu meeting. She called on the women to form an organisation which could send delegates to the soviet. The city-wide organisation which sprang from this meeting became the Union of Soldiers' Wives, established in June. It was dominated by Bolsheviks.

The soldiers' wives also had an impact outside the capital city. In Kazan, in May 1917, a meeting of soldiers' wives was advised to take the grievances to the local soviet. The whole meeting marched to the soviet, which was in session. The soviet sent a representative to pacify the women, and told them to elect a representative to the soviet. The women agreed, but they did not disperse until they had marched around the town with banners and placards. The soviet was compelled to hold a public meeting the following week. It lasted for four hours, finally ending at 1am. The women won the right to cheap firewood and subsidised meals in the local café.[69] In Kherson province, the soldiers' wives requisitioned grain by forcing their way into rich people's houses and taking what they thought was fair. 'The state flour trader who did not want to offer them his goods at discounted prices was beaten by a band of soldiers' wives, and the *pristav*, the local police chief, who wanted to hurry to his help, escaped the same fate by a hair's breadth'.[70]

Militant action and organisation led many soldiers' wives to socialist politics and the women played an important role in the revolutionary movement at a local level.[71] A police report of a meeting of the soldiers' wives in Tambov explained that the soldiers' wives mostly supported the Bolsheviks because of their long-standing opposition to the war and their demand to end it immediately. A liberal woman who had led the committee for the relief of soldiers' wives in the militant Vyborg District of St Petersburg told Krupskaya that the women 'do not trust us; they are displeased with whatever we do; they have faith only in the Bolsheviks'.[72] Leading Bolshevik women saw the potential in the soldier's wives. Who better to carry socialist arguments into the heart of army units than the wives, sisters and mothers of soldiers? Krupskaya remembered, 'The first to carry on Bolshevik agitation among soldiers were the sellers of sunflower seeds, cider etc; many were soldiers' wives.'[73]

The Bolshevik women wanted to express the new radicalism among women and to win the women to socialist politics. The perfect vehicle for this was the paper launched in 1914 and closed down by the censors. They decided to relaunch the Bolshevik women's paper, *Rabotnitsa*, and the first issue appeared on 10 May 1917. A Bolshevik called Vera Slutskaia had returned to Petrograd in March 1917. She realised the potential among the working women she met and convinced the Petrograd Committee to sanction the publication of pamphlets aimed specifically at women. Thus, when the exiled women leaders returned to Russia after the February Revolution, there was a framework already in place to relaunch *Rabotnitsa*.

The first issue of *Rabotnitsa* immediately sold out of 40,000 copies. *Rabotnitsa* rallies overflowed with thousands of women workers. It became the centrepiece of the party's work among women. The paper reached tens of thousands of women. 'The Social Democratic Party is the only party that demands women's equality and fights for it', argued one editorial.[74] The paper attacked male trade union leaders for discriminating against women. One letter from a female factory worker suggested that old attitudes from the villages were still found in the factories. Male factory workers, she wrote, 'are all for equal rights in words, but when it comes to deeds it turns out that the chicken is not a bird, and the Baba [peasant woman] is not a human being'.[75] The paper gave voice to women's demands while arguing for unity between working men and women. Konkordia Samoilova wrote, 'If a woman is capable of climbing the scaffold and fighting on the barricades, then she is capable of being an equal in the workers' family and in workers' organisations'.[76] Another editorial argued, 'The time has passed when the success of the worker's cause will be decided only by organising men'.[77]

The paper brought together some of the great women of the Bolshevik movement, women who were determined that women's liberation should be at the heart of the socialist revolution. Among them were Nadya Krupskaya, Inessa Armand, Konkordia Samoilova and Anna and Maria Ulyanova. Krupskaya addressed huge mixed meetings in Vyborg District; Armand did the same in Moscow.

Rabotnitsa was edited by Samoilova, along with Klavdiia Nikolaeva and Praskovia Kudelli. Lots of working women, and some men, wrote for the paper. It was a tabloid paper which reinforced the Bolsheviks' commitment to women's equality.

But *Rabotnitsa* was more than a paper. It was the organisational centre for Bolshevik work among the women of Petrograd. *Rabotnitsa* was at the centre of networks, collecting information, organising meetings and setting up a school for agitators. Koncordia Samoilova called for *Rabotnitsa* groups to send delegates to soviets, on Lenin's suggestion. *Rabotnitsa* cemented women's relationship with the Bolshevik Party. It was funded by working women's wages; for example, tram operator Alexandra Rodionova donated three days' wages to the paper. During May and June, the Bolsheviks organised a series of *Rabotnitsa* rallies and organising schools to encourage and develop a new cadre of activists around the slogan, 'Down with war, down with high prices'. When anger boiled over into strikes and riots in Petrograd in July

1917, the Provisional Government was able to blame the Bolsheviks and accuse them of being German spies. The government took advantage of the situation to crack down on the revolutionaries, arresting many and forcing others into hiding. When Kollontai was arrested, a meeting of domestic workers called to protest attracted 1,000 women. In the repression of July, no rallies were held, but they were back in August. Some 5,000 attended the August rally and called for the Bolshevik prisoners to be freed. Other rallies demanded an end to the war.

When the Provisional Government had launched a disastrous military offensive in July 1917, *Rabotnitsa* organised a large international meeting calling for opposition to the criminal slaughter of the war and for worldwide workers' solidarity. A huge number of local rallies followed. These networks politicised women agitating in their workplaces and neighbourhoods and created networks of socialists. *Rabotnitsa* helped to pave the way for the October Revolution.

9. 'We carried the Revolution on our shoulders'[78]

On the evening of 10 October 1917, Alexandra Kollontai left her flat wearing an ornate hat and carrying the kind of umbrella that would mark her as a 'lady' to any watchful police spies. She headed for the flat of a party worker, Tatiana Flaxerman, whose husband, Sukhanov, the man who overheard the office girls discussing the possibility of imminent revolution, had agreed to be out for the night. The people Kollontai joined around the dining table in the dimly lit front room were all in disguise; Lenin wore a grey wig. From ten o'clock at night until the next morning, members of the Bolshevik Central Committee delivered their reports, and each report testified to the workers' and soldiers' readiness to fight. Zinoviev and Kamenev opposed the idea that workers should seize power in the name of the soviets, even though the Bolsheviks had won majorities in both the Petrograd and Moscow Soviets with their demand: All Power to the Soviets. 'What did those cowards want?' Alexandra wrote. 'To gain power by the opportunist parliamentary path?'[79]

As dawn broke, the vote was taken, ten to two in favour of the armed uprising. A samovar was brought in and the euphoric but ravenous Bolsheviks ate and drank. They went on to form a special bureau to organise the arming of men and women factory workers, soldiers and sailors. 'Alexandra walked back along the familiar early morning streets and canals in a daze of triumph and tiredness and, going straight to the soviet, delivered a passionate speech calling for an end to power-sharing with the government, and all power to the soviets'.[80]

By October 1917, some 30,000 women had joined the

Bolsheviks. When the party demanded that all power be transferred to the soviets, these women responded. They helped to make the October Revolution and sustain it through the Civil War. The revolution intensified the Bolshevik Party's long-standing practice of involving women in all its activities. The underground years had bred egalitarianism. 'The revolutionary year 1917 was so filled with general ideas of freedom that it quickly became a point of official pride with the Bolsheviks that they had so many women working in their organisation'.[81] Bolsheviks campaigned for women's rights amongst male workers and fought to have female representatives in workplaces where women were a significant presence. The experienced female revolutionaries were able to interact with newly politicised women.

One example was Anna Litveiko, who began work aged 12 and, despite being young, chased her abusive and violent father out of the family home. She heard a Menshevik speaker at her factory but found him too moderate, noting that Menshevik speakers were all intellectuals while the Bolsheviks were workers. She was elected to her factory committee where she met a Bolshevik, Natasha Bogacheva and in 1917, she joined the Bolshevik Party herself. When a foreman at the factory burnt a woman with an iron rod, the women called a meeting, dumped him in a wheelbarrow and drove him out of the factory. During October, Anna and Natasha were active in the revolution, carrying weapons around the city and carrying the wounded to medical points. Other left groups considered women like Anna to be too young to have serious political convictions. Only the Bolsheviks encouraged them to read and to overcome their fear of public speaking to take part in the soviets.

Many of the most prominent Bolshevik women, Kollontai, Armand and Krupskaya, were in exile when the February Revolution began. However, another generation of women played an important role in the Bolshevik Party throughout the revolution. Nina Agadzhanova joined the Bolsheviks in 1907 while a student, was active in building the party in the underground and was arrested five times and exiled twice. In 1917, she was a member of the Vyborg District of the Bolshevik Party. She was also the executive secretary of *Rabotnitsa* and throughout 1917 she was working on underground missions against the White Armies. She later wrote a screenplay on which the film Battleship Potemkin was based.[82]

Women were underrepresented in the leaderships of all the political parties competing for popularity in 1917. American journalist Bessie Beatty wrote, 'Here, as elsewhere, governmental honours were largely awarded to the male; but the mundane business of making [the] world of meat and drink was largely left to women'.[83] She described a democratic convention where of 1,600 delegates only 23 were women. Many other women were there, serving behind the samovars, making sandwiches, taking minutes and counting votes. Beatty commented, 'It was so natural, it almost made me homesick'.[84] Despite this general picture, two women, Alexandra Kollontai and Elena Stasova, were on the Bolshevik Central Committee in 1917, and they were joined a year later by Varvar Yakovleva. Women took up some key roles in the soviet government. Kollontai also occupied a key position in the new government, first as Commissar of Social Welfare and later as Commissar for Propaganda. Inessa Armand and Nadya Krupskaya also had roles in the new government. The first ever woman to lead a national government in modern Europe was Bolshevik Eugenia Bosh, who was leader of the soviet government of Ukraine in 1917. However, many leading women chose not to take up leading positions in the new socialist government.

This absence of women in the new government was the result of several factors. One was without doubt the assumptions made by men about women's capacity to lead others. Another was the attitude of the women themselves to political leadership. Women often choose to occupy lower-profile positions and to work for their cause without seeking the limelight because of their lack of confidence and a perceived lack of experience and education (women had been excluded from higher education in Russia). In addition, many women were still responsible for caring for children and felt that they could not take on high positions and still fulfil their family responsibilities. For all these reasons, women were under-represented in top positions in the Bolshevik Party and in the government.

However, Alexandra Kollontai, who had worked tirelessly to involved women in revolutionary politics, wrote enthusiastically about the number of women active in the soviet government: 'We have women not only as soviet members, but also as presidents in local soviets. Many women act as commissars an all branches of social and State life, and at the front'.[85] It is also worth remembering that in Britain, the first woman was not appointed to a cabinet office until 1929, when Margaret Bondfield was appointed Minister for Labour. The first woman in the US government was Frances Perkins who became Secretary of State for Labour, but not until 1933. The Bolsheviks' failure to appoint more women to key positions should be understood in the context of the time. The revolutionary regime got more women out from behind the samovar than any comparable government at the time.

Beyond the new government, thousands of women threw themselves into supporting the October Revolution. Women were inspired to become revolutionary leaders in the wider movement, among workers and soldiers. One such woman was Rosalya Zemliachka. She came from a radical Jewish family and she was only 15 when she was arrested for the first time. She became a Marxist in 1896 and remained active in the Bolshevik underground until 1917. In February 1917, Zemliachka was the secretary of the Bolsheviks' Moscow City Committee. This was no desk job. Zemliachka was a staunch supporter of Lenin and a determined political operator. When the Moscow

Committee failed to back a seizure of power, Zemliachka and a group of her male comrades broke away and formed their own committee. The two groups came together in October when they defeated the Provisional Government's troops in two days. After the civil war began, Zemliachka volunteered for service at the front and in August 1918 was sent to Belorussia to deal with troops refusing to fight for the Red Army. She gave a rousing speech and spent two weeks persuading the men to fight. Then they boarded the trains to the front. She later became the chief political officer of the Eighth Army in Ukraine. She was a leader who commanded loyalty and respect, and she proved to be a ruthless opponent of the White Armies.[86]

Radicalisation in the army meant that soldiers could be won to socialism by female agitators. By April 1917, Alexandra Kollontai was one of the most popular and prominent Bolsheviks in Petrograd. She was presented to a meeting of soldiers and asked them to delegate her to represent them at the Petrograd Soviet. It took the soldiers a day to get over their shock at being asked to delegate a female Bolshevik; then they voted for her. Liudmilla Stal spent most of 1917 at the naval base of Kronstadt, winning sailors and sailors' wives to socialism. The men would immediately be called on to defend their revolution. The revolutionary regime was attacked by White Armies and foreign powers; the ensuing civil war led to the deaths of some ten million Russians.

A significant number of women joined the Red Army. While men were forcibly conscripted for service in the civil war, women were not required to participate. Nevertheless, they did, in large numbers. An estimated 50,000 to 70,000 women had joined the Red Army by 1920, making up two percent of the overall armed forces. A few women emerged as military leaders. One was Eugenya Bosh. She joined the Bolsheviks in 1901. In 1906, she packed up her daughters, left a note for her husband and headed for Kiev, where she became secretary of the Russian Social Democratic

Group before she was arrested and exiled to Siberia. She escaped abroad, returning to Russia after the February Revolution. In October 1917, Bosh got permission to address a regiment of soldiers stationed in a town in central Ukraine. They were known as 'The Wild Division', and when she arrived they were armed and had been drinking heavily. Undaunted, Bosh spoke for two hours as she explained the need to replace the failing Provisional Government with a soviet government. When she eventually left, their band rushed to find their instruments so that they could see her off in style. A month later the Chief of Staff wrote, expressing the antisemitism which was all too common among army officers, that 'Agitators, such as the Jewess Bosh, have contaminated all the units of the regiment'.[87] Bosh's ability to convince the soldiers that their future lay with socialism was more powerful than the prejudices many must have held against her. The Chief of Staff recognised how dangerous this was for the old order, which had relied for so long on antisemitism and sexism to keep the working class divided and weak.

Shortly afterwards, another regiment stationed 20 miles away at Vinnitsa, mutinied. The army called for reinforcements and Bosh set out to persuade the Wild Division not to respond to the army's command. The soldiers stood packed in a square in the freezing rain listening to her, and the following day she returned to Vinnitsa at the head of a mutinous artillery company intending to join the mutineers instead of crushing them. After a few days of fighting the town fell to Bosh and her rebels. Later, during the civil war, Bosh went on to bring Ukraine under Bolshevik control, earning Victor Serge's description of her as one of the most capable military leaders at the time. A few months later, Bosh launched the Ukrainian Congress of Soviets, which announced a Soviet Republic and she became temporarily the first woman to lead a national government. In January 1918, Bosh became the minister of the interior in the Soviet Republic of Ukraine. After Lenin's death, she became a vocal and principled critic of Stalin's leadership of the party. As a supporter of Trostsky, she became both disillusioned and depressed. In January 1925, when Trotsky was forced out of his position as leader of the Red Army by Stalin, Bosh committed suicide.

10. Legislating for liberation

The Bolsheviks were committed to women's liberation, but their achievements in this area have been hugely underrated by most historians. Life for many Russian peasant women had changed little since the medieval period. The exploitation of women was legally condoned, and men proved their love for their wives by beating them regularly. The whip hung on the wall over the bed in many peasant households.[88] Women's lives were destroyed by multiple pregnancies, miscarriages and high infant mortality rates. They were bought and sold like cattle. They could not inherit or own wealth, and they could not take a job or hold a passport without their husband's permission. In the Muslim east of Russia, the system of bride price or *kalym* echoed the practices followed in the peasant villages in western Russia, where fathers often sold their daughters into arranged marriages. 'A chicken's not a bird and a woman's not a human', one proverb ran, while another went, 'I thought I saw two people walking down the street but it was just a man and his wife'.

German socialist Clara Zetkin visited a Bolshevik women's centre and heard a woman tell her story: 'We were silent slaves. We had to hide in our rooms and cringe before our husbands who were also our lords. Our fathers sold us at the age of ten, even younger. Our husbands would beat us with a stick and whip us when he felt like it. If he wanted to freeze us, we froze. Our daughters, a joy to us and a help around the house, he sold, just as we had been sold'.[89]

The Provisional Government had begun to tackle women's issues. In April 1917, the first All Russian Muslim Women's Congress took place, with 59 delegates meeting in front of 300 women. They debated sharia law, plural marriage, women's rights and the hijab. China Miéville describes how the conference agreed on ten principles, among them: 'women's right to vote, the equality of the sexes, and the non-compulsory nature of the hijab'.[90] While the February Revolution thus ushered in some improvements in women's status, including the right to vote, the October Revolution created an extraordinary body of new laws that aimed not just at equality with men, but at genuine liberation.

The revolutionary regime aimed to smash the chains of patriarchy and male domination. They enacted laws which broke male control over the family and granted women full equality. Six weeks after the revolution, civil marriage was legalised, and divorce was made legal and accessible to all. Kollontai was centrally involved in drafting new legislation and hailed this as a great victory. The marriage ceremony was made simple and Kollontai added a codicil which stated the couple could choose either surname when they married. The Code on Marriage, the Family, and Guardianship was ratified in October 1918. It allowed both spouses to retain rights to their own property and earnings, abolished all distinctions between legitimate and illegitimate children, and made divorce available upon request. Homosexuality was legalised. 'The new family law was without precedent in history', Tariq Ali points out,[91] one of only a handful of socialist and feminist historians who have recognised the extent of the Soviet government's ambitions for women and its extraordinary legislative transformation of the family.[92]

The principle of 'equal pay for equal work' was enshrined in law. By 1920, Russian women had the right to abortion – 53 years before the USA and 47 years before Britain. The Ministry for the Protection of Maternity and Childhood introduced support for working mothers, including 16 weeks paid maternity leave and insurance to pay a friend to take time off to help with the birth. These reforms were way in advance of what women enjoyed in Western European countries. They did not, however, constitute real liberation. At the heart of Marxist writing on women was the idea that women had to be freed from their domestic duties inside the private family unit. While women remained the cooks, laundresses, cleaners and child-rearers in their own families, they could not be equal and free. The Soviet Government thus began to create collective provision which could free women from the burden of childcare and housework. It launched a drive to create communal laundries and canteens to free women from the burden of washing. They established crèches and schools to free women from childcare and enable them to participate in the workforce. By 1919, some 90 percent of Petrograd's population had access to public restaurants, washing facilities and childcare.

The Bolsheviks also launched a movement aimed at empowering women. Under the leadership of Alexandra Kollontai, Inessa Armand and Nadezhda Krupskaya, this movement, the *Zhenotdel*, spread the news of the revolution, enforced its laws and set up political education and literacy classes for working-class and peasant women. One historian has called *Zhenotdel* 'one of the most ambitious attempts to emancipate women ever undertaken by a government'.[93] In the autumn of 1918, over 1,000 women gathered for the first All Russian Women's Congress to hear rousing speeches from Armand, Kollontai and Samoilova. A network of women's committees was established. They argued that working women could be a key resource for the besieged regime and developed ideas about the New Woman, an autonomous and sexually-liberated woman of the future. *Zhenotdel* workers travelled the length and breadth of Russia, taking their message of equality and rights, and facing down violence from men who feared their message. They travelled to Central Asia, wearing veils and organising 'Red Yertas' and 'Red Boats' to reach out to

Muslim women and campaign against illiteracy.

Zhenotdel workers organised women to fight in the Red Army and in guerrilla units. They organised activities, clubs and congresses to encourage women to seek for collective solutions to their problems and to build their confidence. *Zhenotdel* gave women a voice and the hope of a different life. The struggle to uproot centuries of oppression was an enormous one. There were heated debates about whether the revolution in personal lives could be achieved before the economy had developed, about the nature of sexuality and the ideal relationship between the sexes. Tragically, the future the revolutionaries sought could not be constructed in the devastated, war-torn country. The resources necessary to create alternatives to the family were not there. The facilities were inadequate and in short supply. Passing laws was one thing, but changing deeply rooted attitudes, expectations and assumptions was more difficult.

Despite the enormous material difficulties confronting the women of 1917, for a brief few months they provided a glimpse of what a socialist society could offer to women. With the failure of the German and Hungarian Revolutions, Soviet Russia was left isolated and utterly impoverished. The vision of women's liberation could not be made real under such dire circumstances. Although gains proved to be temporary, they achieved more through their revolution than women in other societies achieved through years of more conventional campaigning and protesting. In the process, they bequeathed to us an inspiring vision of how socialism can create the potential for women's liberation. As Kollontai told Bessie Beatty, 'Even if we are conquered, we have done great things. We are breaking the way, abolishing the old ideas'. [94]

11. Leninists, feminists and 'worshipful women'

A group of highly-talented and courageous revolutionaries shared their lives with Vladimir Lenin: Nadya Krupskaya, Inessa Armand, his mother and mother-in-law, and his three sisters, Anna, Olga and Maria, as well as fellow revolutionaries like Kollontai and his large staff of secretaries. They are given passing mentions in biographies of Lenin where they are invariably described as 'worshipful, subservient women'.[95] They have generally been treated by historians as if they were mere appendages of Lenin, minor planets orbiting his glowing sun. However, the women in his circle had all come to politics independently of Lenin. They had endured imprisonment and exile, lived abroad and worked in the revolutionary underground movement. At key moments, they provided Lenin with vital material and practical support. Anna and Maria Ulyanova, for example, kept contact with Lenin when he was exiled and published his writings. They also gave him political support at key moments in the revolutionary process. It is inconceivable that the women who shared his political aspirations, his life and his home would not have had political influence on him or any distinctive ideas of their own.

August 1914 was a disaster for the international socialist movement. The mighty German Social Democratic Party ignored years of pledges to oppose imperialist war and voted to support its own government. The collapse of internationalism was a terrible shock to those determined to oppose war. In Germany, Rosa Luxemburg and Clara Zetkin were devastated and isolated. Russian revolutionaries formed a tight knit group of anti-war activists, including Anna and Maria Ulyanova, Nadya Krupskaya, Armand, Kollontai and Lenin. Kollontai and Armand were the driving force behind the first international anti-war gathering, the Bern Conference of 1915.

When Lenin was told of the February Revolution, one of the first things he did was to write to Kollontai, outlining the need for an international proletarian revolution and a seizure of power. She recalled being thrilled by his ideas and she rushed to Petrograd to argue for the revolutionary slogan, Bread, Peace and Land. Lenin arrived at the Finland Station in April 1917 and his speech attacking the Provisional Government caused huge shock and outrage among Bolsheviks as well as other socialists. In his first speech to the Petrograd Soviet outlining the need for further revolution in Russia, he was heckled and shouted down.

Kollontai was the only Bolshevik at that meeting to publicly endorse Lenin's April Theses. 'Nadezhda Krupskaya and Inessa Armand, smiling at her from the front row, provided her only support. From most of the others present, her words provoked cat calls and jeers, and in the bourgeois press her speech earned her the title of "Valkyrie of the Revolution"'.[96] Kollontai recalled, 'I was the only one to stand up for Lenin's view against a whole series of hesitant Bolsheviks'.[97] Others thought he was delirious or insane. Russia was too poor and too backward to contemplate a socialist revolution, they argued. The Russian bourgeoisie must be allowed to develop Russia before socialism was a possibility. Lenin and his supporters argued that the Russian Revolution could be the spark that could ignite the world socialist revolution.

The same group were united in October at the crucial moment of insurrection. Kollontai was in the Central Committee meeting that voted to seize power. On the eve of the revolution, on 24 October, Lenin was frustrated by the party's lack of action. He resolved to reach over the heads of the Central Committee to the district Bolshevik committees. He insisted that his draft appeal be delivered only to Krupskaya to disseminate to party members. The final sentence read, 'The government is tottering. It must be given the deathblow at all costs. To delay action is fatal.'[98]

This group of women supported Lenin at key moments and they helped him to formulate strategies that would involve the vast potential among the working women. The rise of the feminist movement in Russia meant that many socialists were hostile to any idea of women organising separately. Krupskaya certainly opposed the idea of a women's bureau during the First World War. However, the experience of workers' struggles changed this. Firstly, when a crisis in employment in September 1917 led to men calling for women to be sacked first and paid less, the Bolsheviks opposed them. They realised that as women were now such a large component of the working class, such a move would divide and weaken the whole trade union movement. Secondly, female workers had proved that they were capable of both militancy and organisation. The women had fought to improve their immediate conditions, and for wider political change. They had won the right to play a role in trade unions and in socialist organisations.

The women close to Lenin were among the first and most enthusiastic campaigners for women's equality. Lenin was committed to making women's equality a central strand of the RSDLP from its inception. He was sympathetic to calls for political work among women and he supported the establishment of both *Zhenotdel* and *Rabotnitsa*. His speeches on women and to women and his conversations with Clara Zetkin reveal him to be deeply committed to the project of women's liberation from the drudgery of domestic labour. He spoke at the first Women's Congress and supported all the initiatives aimed at women workers. It was often said that the Russian Revolution could not have triumphed without Lenin. We could add that Lenin would not have triumphed without the women who supported him and helped to formulate his ideas and put them into practice.

Conclusion: Tribunes of the oppressed

Katy Turton, biographer of Lenin's sisters, suggests that women disappeared in 1917, leaving only Kollontai visible on the podium. She suggests that the women lacked confidence and that the older generation was deeply committed to serving the movement and valued self-sacrifice and humility.[99] Amongst Bolsheviks, women were encouraged to participate fully in public life and revolutionary activities and to write about their work. However, Bolshevism also reinforced the idea that women should not promote themselves in their writing, for Bolsheviks believed that revolutionaries of both sexes should portray themselves as modest servants of the cause. Asserting individual achievement was not compatible with the Communists' ideology of collective endeavour. Some women who had spent years in clandestine work would have found the transition to mass agitation a political challenge. Others had been denied the right to higher education and felt unable to develop theoretically. Kollontai was certainly the most visible of the female Bolsheviks, but she was not alone. Elena Stasova, for example, occupied a key position as secretary to the Central Committee. She was responsible for party correspondence, financial records and distributing money.

It is true, however, that the women who did not disappear in 1917 would disappear within a few years, as Stalin strengthened his grip on power. 'Old Bolsheviks' were dangerous to Stalin because they knew that Stalin had not led the 1917 Revolution and that Lenin had never looked on Stalin as his heir. Of those who accompanied Lenin on the sealed train in

April 1917, only Krupskaya died of old age. She was bullied and slandered into silence, her memoirs of Lenin unpublished until she had purged Trotsky from her writing. Zinoviev was shot in 1936. He confessed to his 'crimes', believing that this would save his family. It did not. His son, Stephan, who was a child on the sealed train in April 1917, was shot in 1938. His wife, Zlata Zinovieva, was exiled, and then shot, also in 1938. Olga Ravich spent 20 years exiled in the Arctic camps and died of lung cancer in 1957. Her writing on education and her children's books were all banned under Stalin. Karl Radek and Grigory Sokolnikov, who were also passengers on the train, stood trial together in January 1937. They were sentenced to labour camps where they were both beaten to death.

Other Old Bolsheviks suffered the same fate. In 1936 Lev Kamenev also 'confessed' his guilt in an effort to save his family. It also failed. Olga Kamenev's 17-year old son was executed in 1938, and she was shot in 1941, alongside Maria Spiridonova. A painting by Soviet artist Mikhail Sokolo still hanging in a Moscow museum shows Lenin arriving at the Finland Station in April 1917 and behind him on the steps is Joseph Stalin. This is artistic fake news: Stalin was not there. The people who embodied the revolutionary experience had been eradicated and Stalinist myths erected in their place.

The Bolshevik Party was made up of individuals with their own strengths and weaknesses, who adhered to different currents within the party. Those men and women who wanted to find new ways to engage with working women often faced scepticism and hostility. Despite its flaws, however, the Bolshevik Party provided women with an outlet for their revolutionary aspirations: 'Nowhere in law abiding Russia could women find a life so emancipated from the constraints of their nation's patriarchal traditions.'[100] The party was shaped by the women who threw off centuries of oppression to strike and organise, just as the party provided the ideas that the women needed to win their liberation.

Historian Barbara Clements calls Kollontai, Armand, Krupskaya, Stasova, Anna and Maria Ulyanov 'Bolshevik Feminists'.[101] In fact, they were Bolsheviks who developed their party's theory and practice in opposition both to bourgeois feminism, which ignored class, and in opposition to the kind of Marxism which told women not to divide the working class and to wait for the revolution to triumph before they raised their demands. They were revolutionaries who understood that women faced a double burden of oppression and exploitation and could be won to revolutionary politics. They encouraged their comrades to challenge the ideas that perpetuated women's oppression, wherever those ideas were expressed. The working women who made the Russian Revolution repaid their confidence and their efforts in full.

Section Two
Revolutionary Lives

Anna (1864–1935) and Maria Ulyanova (1878-1937)

Anna and Maria, who were respectively Lenin's older and younger sister, are rarely remembered by historians of the revolution. Valentinov, a revolutionary who first met Lenin in 1904, wrote that he was like 'the sun in the planetary system', whom Maria 'almost idolised' and Anna saw as 'an oracle'.[102] It was, of course, Lenin who is said to have introduced his grateful sisters to Marxism. A contemporary of Anna's later wrote, 'Under the influence of reading and conversations with Vladimir Ilyich, a Marxist outlook began to take shape in Anna'.[103]

Biographies of Lenin tend to refer to his sisters only during his childhood and the early revolutionary period, and then during his final illness when Maria cared for him. The women barely feature in most accounts of the Russian Revolution and when they do, highly gendered language is often used. For example, Robert Service described Maria, who never married, as 'a crabby spinster'.[104] Others described Anna's husband Mark as hen-pecked, with Service speculating that he often felt the lash of his wife's tongue. According to Service's account, his sisters' adoration generated Lenin's tyrannical tendencies:

> *He had been surrounded by what might be called an aura of warmly expectant encouragement. It was to give him a general presumption that others should indulge his wishes. Thus he appeared a 'natural leader'. But it also limited his awareness of the difficulties he caused. He was so used to getting his way that, if balked in any fashion, he was altogether too likely to throw a fit of anger. He absolutely hated being thwarted. As a young man he belatedly became a sort of spoiled child nurtured by four women.*[105]

Yet Anna, who was the oldest child, was active in Marxist circles for years before Lenin joined her. Both

Anna and Maria were committed revolutionaries for their whole lives. From the 1890s to 1917, Anna and Maria operated as revolutionaries independently of Lenin. They used their own political beliefs and judgement, as well as their experience and skill as revolutionaries. Anna and Maria worked closely with many leading Bolsheviks, including Bukharin, Lunacharsky and Stasova. Like many revolutionaries, Anna and Maria lived nomadic lives during the underground years, travelling extensively around Russia and Europe, often to carry out party duties, but also to escape arrest and sometimes to serve terms of exile. Anna and Maria continued with their revolutionary agitation when they were in danger of arrest and even from their prison cells. They also agitated tirelessly amongst workers, soldiers and prisoners.

Anna and Maria were central to the production of the Bolshevik Party's newspapers and publications, which were crucial to the Social-Democratic movement. Papers enabled the circulation of news and ideas between members of the party and were one of the few threads holding disparate and geographically far-flung revolutionary groups together. Anna and Maria had a hand in the publication of all the major newspapers of the underground period. They both played a prominent role in producing the RSDLP's key publication, the paper Iskra. Anna helped establish the newspaper while abroad between 1900 and 1902, working for Iskra organisations, first in Paris and then Berlin. She also wrote articles for the newspaper. Maria began working for Iskra in Moscow, receiving the newspaper hidden in the covers of books sent from abroad. As one historian put it, during the underground years 'there were no trivial and no great deeds, when the great work depended on the trivialities, when a careless step could lead to the collapse of the organisation, when everything might crash down because of a trifling [matter]'.[106]

Alexander Ulyanov, the older son of the Ulyanov family,

was executed in March 1887 for attempting to assassinate Tsar Alexander III. Anna and Alexander were members of the same groups and attended the same meetings and demonstrations. On the night Alexander attempted the assassination his flat was searched and a telegram to Anna was discovered. She was also arrested. When Alexander was sentenced to death, Anna was sentenced to exile. Anna's mother successfully campaigned for Anna to be allowed to serve her sentence at the family's estate rather than abroad. From 1893, both Anna and Maria consistently involved themselves in the underground, illegal revolutionary movement. Anna escaped arrest in 1900 by going to France and Germany where she joined local Social-Democratic groups and often visited Lenin in Geneva and Munich. In January 1904 both Anna and Maria were arrested and spent months in prison. In the summer of 1905 Maria arrived in St Petersburg and joined Anna in the hectic work of the Bolshevik Committee there. After the defeat of the 1905 Revolution, Maria endured numerous periods of exile and built socialist organisation in the towns to which she was sent. Anna, who had married and adopted a son, travelled around Russia and edited and organised underground publications such as *Rabotnitsa*.

In 1917, Anna and Maria threw themselves into revolutionary activity. Maria acquired a typewriter and began writing slogans for distribution around Petrograd. Both sisters began to work for the relaunched *Rabotnitsa*: Anna managed to get 12,000 copies of the first edition of *Rabotnitsa* printed and distributed and was able to get seven issues in total printed between 23 February and 26 June 1917. On 8 March they joined the Bolshevik Party's Central Committee. Anna and Maria wrote an article about the February Revolution in *Pravda*: 'How quickly everything has come to pass! Like a story, like a fantasy – beautiful and solemn. In one day more has been lived through, than at any other time would be experienced in a year, and in a few days the masses have rid us of the past.'[107]

Between 1917 and 1924 Anna and Maria both occupied high-level posts in the Bolshevik regime. Anna helped to establish and then became the head of the Department of the Protection of Childhood, while Maria became the executive secretary of Pravda and the leader of the *Rabsel 'kor*, a workers' organisation.

Police reports from before the revolution provide a good description of Anna and Maria's status in the Bolshevik organisation. They referred to Anna as Elizarova: '[Elizarova] is a person of extremely harmful tendencies. Using her foreign contacts she gives assistance to the introduction of illegal literature to the limits of the Empire, communicates information about events in Russia to foreign revolutionary activists and underground publications, and gives support and services to revolutionary organisations. In view of Elizarova's serious significance, the Department of Police asks that she be put under police surveillance'.[108]

A separate report described Maria and the rest of the family: 'Mariia Il'inichna undoubtedly upholds the revolutionary tradition of her family, who are distinguished by an extremely harmful tendency. Her brother, Aleksandr, was executed in 1887 for his participation in a terrorist conspiracy, Vladimir has been sent to Siberia for treason, and Dmitrii was recently put under police surveillance for the propagation of Social-Democratic ideas. Sister Anna is in constant contact with foreign agents and is, like her husband Mark Timofeevich Elizarov, under police surveillance'.[109]

Nadezhda Krupskaya (1869-1939)

Nadezhda (Nadya) Krupskaya is often portrayed as nothing more than Lenin's loyal wife and helper. Russian historian Dimitri Volkogonov described Krupskaya as Lenin's shadow and described how her life had, 'meaning only because she was linked to him'.[110] Krupskaya's subservient role is asserted and reasserted. Her biographer, Robert H McNeal, did not consider it necessary to provide any supporting evidence: 'Krupskaya obviously worked under Lenin's direct supervision, and there is no point in trying to inflate her independent role'.[111] In fact, Krupskaya was a committed revolutionary socialist before she met Lenin.

Nadya Krupskaya was born to a noble but impoverished family. Contemporaries noticed how from her childhood she was inspired with a spirit of protest. She won the gold medal at school but, as a woman, was excluded from higher education. She began to participate in several discussion circles and she was already a Marxist when she first met Vladimir Lenin in 1894. In October 1896 Krupskaya was arrested for the first time and she was permitted to join Lenin in exile in Siberia on condition that they married.

Krupskaya's mother, Elizaveta Vasilevna Krupskaya went with her daughter. She became a permanent fixture in her daughter's life in exile. References to Elizaveta are scant although she does feature in an article called 'What Lenin Ate'. Helen Rappaport described this first period of exile, saying Lenin was, 'glad of the companionship of Nadya, and even of his mother-in-law'.[112] When they travel, the mother-in-law is always described as in tow. Mothers-in-law are an unwelcome drag, she implies, yet, since Elizaveta complained about Lenin's grumpiness, perhaps it was she who was putting up with him. Elizaveta abandoned her deeply held religious faith during her exile. She decoded Bolshevik Party correspondence and sewed clothes with special pockets for smuggling documents. To historians, Elizaveta, a woman who left her home and lived with the exiled revolutionaries in Geneva, Paris, Brussels, Galicia and London is a drudge, a dogsbody, a nagging mother-in-law, but never a woman in her own right.

In 1900 Krupskaya published a pamphlet, *The Woman Worker*, aimed at working women. The pamphlet explained how paid work could free women from the control of tyrannical fathers and husbands. A future socialist society would liberate women from the drudgery of child rearing. This could only be achieved, Krupskaya argued, if women engaged in political struggle, 'hand in hand with men in the worker's cause'. She had read Engels' *The Origin of the Family, Private Property and the State*, as well as volume one of Marx's *Capital* as a student but that does not stop her biographer McNeal suggesting that the pamphlet shows how Krupskaya had become a Marxist only under 'Lenin's tutelage'.[113]

On her release from exile in 1901 Krupskaya joined Lenin abroad and with Elizaveta they spent the next five years mixing with emigres in Munich, Paris and London. Krupskaya was not a very good cook, Rappaport tells us, assuming that it was her job: 'Volodya [Lenin] endured Nadya's attempts at home cooking with surprisingly good grace'.[114] Krupskaya had better things to do. She was anything but a mere functionary of the Bolshevik group. Leon Trotsky described how Krupskaya was at the very centre of the party's work; 'she received comrades when they arrived, instructed them when they left, established connections, supplied secret addresses, wrote letters, and coded and decoded correspondence. In her room there was always a smell of burned paper from the secret letters she heated over the fire to read'.[115] Following the 1905 Revolution, Krupskaya returned to St Petersburg where she became secretary of the Central Committee and took over control of the party's finances. The Social Democratic Party grew several times over before the revolutionary tide subsided and she was once again forced into exile.

Krupskaya was one of the first Marxists to attempt to formulate a socialist theory of education. After a period of study, she wrote a short book, *Public Education and Democracy* (1915) in which she outlined the role of labour in education. The book was not published until 1917, when it was reprinted several times. In the summer of 1917, she became a member of the Vyburg Bolshevik

Committee where she developed a network of public schools. When Krupskaya approached a 15-year old, Liza Drabkina, to start a playground, the younger woman told Krupskaya that she, 'wanted to complete the revolution, not wipe kids' noses'. This young activist had grasped an important truth: that women active in socialist politics were often put in charge of areas of work which conformed to ideas of women's role in looking after and educating children. Krupskaya explained that what they were doing was nevertheless vital to winning workers to the Bolshevik Party.[116]

Krupskaya became chair of the Vyborg Committee for Relief of Soldier's Wives. This, McNeal writes, 'was essentially non-party, welfare activity' which was 'certainly not very Leninist'.[117] This is completely wrong. The soldiers' wives were fiercely opposed to the war and were becoming increasingly militant. Thanks to the work of women Bolsheviks like Krupskaya, the soldiers' wives played an important role in supporting the October Revolution. In August 1917, Krupskaya was a delegate to the Sixth Party Congress in Petrograd while Lenin was in hiding. On 5 October she was one of a seven-person delegation from the Vyborg District to the Bolshevik Central Committee, a delegation which argued in support of the seizure of power. She was in Vyborg when the revolution took place some three weeks later.

After the revolution, Krupskaya was the driving force behind a government organisation that aimed to eradicate illiteracy among adults and set up libraries. Krupskaya had never written much and she had avoided public speaking. Now, at the age of 48, she became a prolific author of pamphlets and articles and an orator who travelled around Russia, speaking to meetings of peasants and workers arguing for education. Krupskaya was appointed deputy to Anatoly Lunacharsky, the People's Commissar for Education, where she took charge of the Adult Education Division. McNeal writes that she, 'hurled herself at a furious pace into the impossible task of designing and constructing a human, cultivated socialist system of education in a country that was economically ruined, racked by civil war'.[118]

Despite this economic ruin, Krupskaya helped to transform the education system with a tenfold increase in spending. Free and universal access to education was mandated for all children from the ages of three to sixteen years old, and the number of schools at least doubled within the first two years of the revolution. Co-education was immediately implemented as a means of combating sex discrimination, and for the first time, schools were created for students with learning and other disabilities. Literacy campaigns were launched nationally among toddlers, soldiers, adolescents, workers, and peasants. There were attempts to provide universal crèches and preschools. In the Red Army, illiteracy rates decreased from 50 percent to only 14 percent three years later, and eight percent one year after that. University lectures were opened to workers, and libraries were built, which were staffed by trained librarians.

Krupskaya was a central figure in the Soviet campaign to liberate the minds of Russian workers. A whole new educational system was created in which traditional education was thrown out and new, innovative techniques were implemented which emphasized self-activity, collectivism, and choice, and that drew on students' prior experience, knowledge, and interaction with the real world. This was a huge achievement. Krupskaya is the most patronised and underestimated of all the female Bolsheviks. She survived for some 15 years after Lenin's death in 1924, during which time she both defended Lenin's legacy and compromised with Stalin in order to survive. This later history does not negate the crucial role Krupskaya played in the underground years of the Bolshevik Party and how she dedicated her life to the struggle for a better world. Krupskaya deserves to be recognised as a revolutionary in her own right.

Alexandra Kollontai (1872-1952)

Alexandra Kollontai is the best known of the women Bolsheviks. Historians tend to dwell on her glamour, her unconventional love life and her theories about sexual freedom. However, Kollontai was a revolutionary leader, an activist and speaker not only in Russia but also in Germany, Belgium, France, Britain, Scandinavia and the US. Like Inessa Armand, she was fluent in several languages. Kollontai was one of the most dynamic figures in the Bolshevik Party. She had the courage and determination to shape the party, to propel it towards the women of the working class and to develop the theory and practice of women's liberation.

Kollontai was born into an aristocratic family. Like so many other idealistic young radicals, she began teaching evening classes for workers in St Petersburg. In 1895, she read August Bebel's *Woman and Socialism* and it became a major influence on her. By 1898 Kollontai was a committed Marxist. She left her husband and son to study economics in Zurich, just as Rosa Luxemburg did, and, like Luxemburg, Kollontai published a polemic against Eduard Bernstein's revisionism which was unfortunately suppressed by the censors. In 1899 she began working for the RSDLP in the underground movement. Kollontai was active in the 1905 Revolution and she became one of the Bolsheviks' best-known and most popular speakers and a tireless agitator for revolution.[119] She opposed the majority of the Bolsheviks' strategy of boycotting elections to the Tsarist Duma which she thought could be used as a platform (this was also the view argued by Lenin within the Bolsheviks), a position with which the majority would later come to agree.

From 1905 to 1908 Kollontai led a campaign to organise women workers to fight for their own interests, against employers, against bourgeois feminism, and where necessary against sexism in socialist organisations. She was forced into exile in 1908 and she spent the next nine years writing, teaching, speaking and organising in the international socialist movement. In 1914 Kollontai left Germany in disgust after the German Social Democrat Party voted to support the First World War. She was imprisoned in Sweden and on her release, she made her way to Norway. Kollontai had long supported the Mensheviks but the experience of 1914 brought her closer to the Bolsheviks and she joined them in 1915. She was a primary organiser of the Zimmerwald Conference against the war in 1915, and her pamphlet *Who Needs War?* was translated into several languages.

Kollontai returned to Russia in April 1917, carrying letters from Lenin to the party. From the moment of her arrival, she campaigned against the Provisional Government, in opposition to the majority of Bolsheviks. She was elected to the executive committee of the Petrograd Soviet, after being delegated by an army unit. At a tumultuous meeting of Social Democrats on 4 April, she was the only speaker, other than Lenin, to support the demand for 'All Power to the Soviets'. In October 1917, Kollontai participated in the decision to launch an armed uprising against the government. She was elected Commissar of Social Welfare in the new Soviet government and tried to ease the suffering of orphans in Petrograd's notorious 'Angel Factories'. In 1918 Kollontai led delegations to Sweden, England and France and she played a key role in organizing the First All-Russian Congress of Working and Peasant Women. Despite suffering from a heart attack, Kollontai kept up a gruelling schedule of meetings, speeches and writing. Kollontai, Armand and Krupskaya established the Women's Section or *Zhenotdel*, which she led after Armand's death in 1920.

Alexandra Kollontai was not only a powerful orator, she was a historian of the working-class women's movement in Russia and a theoretician who developed a Marxist approach to the family and sexuality. She described how the private family structure was at the heart of women's oppression and how the family was being undermined by the demands of factory production. In a prescient passage from 1920 she described the pressures that capitalist production placed on the traditional family:

> *The family breaks down as more and more women go out to work. How can one talk about family life when the man and woman work different shifts, and where the wife does not even have the time to prepare a decent meal for her offspring? How can one talk of parents when the mother and father are out working all day and cannot find a few minutes to spend with their children?*[120]

Kollontai also wrote powerfully how women working outside the home and engaging in class struggle could transform themselves. She wrote of 1905, 'At a time of unrest and strike actions, the proletarian woman, downtrodden, timid and without rights, suddenly grows and learns to stand tall and straight.'[121]

Kollontai was also interested in the psychological effects of oppression on both women and men. In *Sexual Relations and the Class Struggle*, written in 1921, she described the spiritual loneliness that afflicts people in a capitalist society based on individualism and egoism. She explained how this forces us to seek a soul mate to possess exclusively, a lover who can, 'charm away the gloom of inescapable loneliness',[122] but this sexual love is based on the submission of women and hypocritical double standards. Sexual freedom, she argued, required women to be freed from the drudgery of housework and for women and men to establish new relationships based on equality, comradeship, respect and freedom. Such relationships, she believed, would be more joyful and fulfilling for both sexes.

This inspiring vision depended on resources to create

social alternatives to the family. However, Russia had endured terrible losses during the First World War and even more in the Civil War which followed the revolution and the revolution failed to spread to other countries. The material resources to create alternatives to the private family did not exist. Kollontai protested against the bureaucratisation of the soviets and of the Communist Party (the Bolshevik Party was renamed in 1918). In 1921 Kollontai published a pamphlet, *The Worker's Opposition* but her criticism ended in 1922 when factions in the Communist Party were banned. Kollontai then became a diplomat spending many years out of Russia as an ambassador to Mexico, Sweden and Norway, returning to Moscow in 1945.

Neither the ultimate failure of the Soviet government to make real its aspiration for women's liberation nor her later compromises with Stalin's regime should undermine what Kollontai achieved during the 1917 Revolution and its immediate aftermath. Despite serious disagreements with Lenin, she was with him at the crucial points of August 1914 and April and October 1917. If she had been a man, her experience, ability, charisma and large body of written work would have assured her a place among the great leaders of the revolution.

Elena Stasova (1873-1966)

Elena Stasova was one of the most respected of the women Bolshevik Party members. She was born in 1873 into a rich, cultivated family (her grandfather had been architect to Tsars Alexander I and Nicholas I). Like many other radicals, she taught workers at St Petersburg's Sunday schools, where she came into contact with Marxists. By 1895 Stasova was smuggling messages to political prisoners and hiding leaflets in her flat. She joined the Russian Social Democrats when the organisation was first established in 1898 and soon became a professional revolutionary. When the RSDLP split into Bolshevik and Menshevik factions in 1903, Stasova sided with Lenin and became a professional revolutionary. She distributed the paper, *Iskra*, in St Petersburg where she was the Bolshevik Party secretary and occupied other leading party positions.

Stasova left Russia for Geneva in 1905 and returned to Russia in 1906 where she directed the Bolshevik Party in Georgia. Stasova was elected to the Bolshevik Party Central Committee in 1912 but was arrested the following year and exiled to Siberia. In 1917 she was appointed secretary to the Bolshevik Central Committee and she became a full member from 1918. She left the Central Committee in 1920 and began working for the Comintern, the Bolshevik Party's international organisation. She spent many years as the Comintern's representative in Germany. Stasova returned to Russia where she worked on the editorial staff of a literary magazine until she retired. Elena Stasova was one of very few old Bolsheviks to survive the rise of Stalin unscathed, perhaps because she first lived abroad and then focused on literature rather than politics.

Inessa Armand (1874-1920)

Inessa Armand has been treated particularly badly by historians who fail to get beyond 'did they, didn't they' speculation about whether she slept with Lenin. Helen Rappaport like many others, contrasts glamorous, confident Armand with dowdy, servile Krupskaya. 'Inessa was everything that Nadezhda Krupskaya was not. She was beautiful, sophisticated, multilingual, as well as being elegant and feminine in an instinctively French way'.[123] And Inessa could even cook, unlike Krupskaya who had also let herself go and was shapeless and slovenly. Thus is created and recreated the tired narrative of a love triangle involving the downtrodden wife, the sophisticated lover and, at the apex, the powerful man.

Historians are unanimous in their view that sexual

attraction must follow conventional beauty. Kollontai's novel *The Great Love* is said to be based on the love triangle between Lenin, Krupskaya and Armand. It seems that the spirit of fiction has informed discussion of their private lives ever since. Even writers who are committed to giving women recognition for their role in revolutionary activity are not immune. For example, Tariq Ali's account of Armand and Lenin's first encounter, in an idyllic Parisian spring, reads a little like a romantic novel. Ali chides Armand's biographer for denying a sexual relationship between her and Lenin, suggesting that only this would make it worth writing a biography of her.[124]

Armand was written out of history by Stalin-era historians who sought to re-establish a traditional moral perspective. Western historians approach Armand through the prism of her relationships with Lenin. She is Lenin's Cudgel, or Lenin's Lieutenant. Historian Ralph Carter Elwood calls her 'Lenin's Girl Friday'.[125] Armand's political activity is always described in relation to Lenin. She 'represents Lenin at an international conference', she goes 'on Lenin's behalf' to rebuild the Bolshevik Party organisation in St Petersburg in 1912. Armand is apparently motivated by loyalty to a man, not her own political convictions. No revolutionary man would be described in these terms.

In fact, Armand was an experienced revolutionary before she met Lenin. She spoke four languages fluently and had the confidence and depth of understanding to speak at international socialist conferences as well as being the only woman to lecture a party school in 1911. She worked closely with Lenin and Krupskaya to build the Bolshevik Party and she fiercely opposed him when she disagreed with him. They argued over a plan for an article she planned to write in 1915 in which supported free love, free both from material constraints and from repressive morality. She also took a very critical view of Brest-Litovsk

Peace Treaty. This educated, sophisticated and dedicated revolutionary was certainly something more than Lenin's Girl Friday.

Armand became a committed revolutionary at the age of thirty and from that point until her death she was a committed activist. Born in Paris in 1874, she was the daughter of a French opera singer and a Russian aristocrat. She was brought up by her Russian grandmother in Moscow. She married a rich French Russian, Alexander Armand, at the age of 19 and had four children. Armand began her political life as a feminist. In 1901, she was refused permission by the Moscow authorities to open a school for girls. The following year she opened a shelter for 'downtrodden women' as part of a wider campaign to rehabilitate Moscow's many prostitutes. When philanthropy proved to be less than satisfying, many women looked to win increased political rights for their sex. Armand, however, was travelling on a different political trajectory. Her experience among the poorest women on Moscow's streets propelled her to the realisation that political rights would not be enough and that the whole political and economic system would have to be changed to win lasting improvements in women's lives.

At the age of 28, Armand left Alexander and went to live with his younger brother Vladimir, who was a revolutionary, and had a child with him. She remained on excellent terms with Alexander Armand, who continued to support her until the end of her life. Through her relationship with Vladimir Armand, she met revolutionaries and read their literature. In 1903 she joined the RSDLP and began to work in the underground. For the next 15 years she tried to combine her political life with spending time with her children. Well-dressed and travelling with four young children, Armand was in an ideal position to smuggle documents across the border from Switzerland into Russia in the false bottom of her children's trunk.

In 1905, some historians believe that she took part in the Moscow uprising, although her biographer believes she was abroad with Vladimir, who suffered from TB. She was arrested in June 1905 and released thanks to Alexander's intercession. She was arrested again in April 1907 and this time, despite Alexander's appeals, she was exiled to northern Russia in November. She escaped a year later and hurried to Switzerland to nurse Vladimir, who died in her arms two weeks later. Armand then travelled to Paris, where she first met Krupskaya and Lenin. She was to share the next seven years of her exile with them.

Armand wanted to develop her theoretical understanding of politics and she taught at a party school in Geneva in 1911 alongside Lenin, Zinoviev and Kamenev. In 1911, she also became the main organiser of the committee that coordinated all the Bolshevik groups across Europe. Armand returned to Russia in 1912 to argue the editors of *Pravda* round to Lenin's perspective. She was arrested, and again she escaped, but not before she helped to steer the Bolshevik Party's paper to respond to the needs and demands of the growing female workforce in Moscow. It was Armand who approached Konkordia Samoilova and Zlata Lilina Zinovieva with her proposal to launch a magazine for women. The scheme developed into *Rabotnitsa*.

Armand opposed the First World War, organising anti-war conferences and publishing publications including *Rabotnitsa*. Bertram Wolfe wrote, 'Inessa continued to play an important part in Lenin's wartime activities. She served on the Bolshevik delegations to Zimmerwald and Kienthal. At the Bern Conference of Bolsheviks she was one of a committee of three, with Zinoviev and Lenin, which drafted the official resolution on war.' He comments that, 'There is no doubt that the real author was Lenin' but he does not explain why this is so beyond doubt.[126] She represented Lenin at the Brussels Unity Conference in

1914, where the Bolsheviks argued for revolutionaries to break away from socialists who supported the war.

In 1917, Armand became secretary to the Moscow Soviet and pushed through reforms to benefit women. Armand was vital to establishing the first Congress for working women in 1918. From this congress the Women's Department, or *Zhenotdel*, was set up, enabling Armand to organise communal facilities such as laundries, canteens and crèches. Armand was appointed head of the women's section of the Central Committee and she launched a paper aimed at women, *Kommunista*. The fifth edition of the paper carried her obituary. After becoming exhausted by working 16-hour days she went to recuperate at a sanatorium in the Caucasus Mountains. She was evacuated when the area came under attack by White armies. She left the train to buy bread and milk and contracted cholera. She died on 23 September 1920, aged 46. She was buried in Red Square with mass singing of the Internationale; one of very few women of the time to be accorded a state funeral.

Konkordia 'Natasha' Samoilova (1876-1921)

Konkordia Samoilova was the daughter of a priest. She took part in her first demonstration in February 1897 while a student in St Petersburg. In 1901, she was expelled from college and spent three months in prison after banned books and a revolver were found during a search of her rooms. The following year she left for Paris to study Marxism and in 1903 she joined the Bolsheviks and became active in the underground movement and adopted the code name Natasha. She was arrested four times between 1902 and 1913, and spent over a year in prison. In 1905 she travelled to Moscow to be part of the insurrection which took place there. Samoilova was a founder editor of *Pravda* and knew how to write and distribute illegal material. Samoilova married in 1913 and, unusually among the women Bolsheviks, she had two children. While conducting Bolshevik agitation amongst railworkers she was attacked by women who accused her of trying to steal their husbands. This convinced her that the revolutionaries must reach out to working women.

In 1913 Samoilova persuaded a reluctant St Petersburg Bolshevik Committee to support a meeting of women to commemorate the new International Women's Day. She was elated when thousands turned up, filling the overflow room and listening attentively to stories of sexual harassment, low pay and hazardous working conditions. Samoilova had ten years' experience as a Bolshevik activist behind her, but it was this meeting which inspired her to devote her activity to women workers and she became one of the Bolsheviks' most inspirational female activists. She was an editor of *Rabotnitsa* in both 1914 and 1917. At the First All-Russian Women's Congress in November 1918, she sat on the podium with Inessa Armand and Alexandra Kollontai. Samoilova died of cholera in 1921.

Olga Kameneva (1883-1941)

Olga Kameneva was Trotsky's sister. She was born in 1883 and joined the RSDLP in 1902. She married Lev Kamenev and in 1908 she began a long period in exile Geneva and Paris. She and her husband became close to Lenin and Krupskaya. Olga Kameneva contributed to editing the main Bolshevik magazine, *Proletariy*. In January 1914 the couple moved back to St Petersburg where Lev Kamenev took charge of the party newspaper, *Pravda*.

After the October Revolution, Olga Kameneva was put in charge of the Theatre Division of the People's Commissariat for Education. Theatre was seen as a very important means by which to reach workers who were illiterate. Kameneva tried to radicalise Russian theatre, but in the spring 1919 she was dismissed from her post by Anatoly Lunacharsky who favoured more traditional theatre. Kameneva was also a member of the board of directors of the *Zhenotdel*.

Kameneva went on to become a leading member of a commission for fighting famine. Her most important role was as the chair of the Society for Cultural Relations with Foreign Countries enabling her to welcome important cultural figures to Russia. Although her marriage broke down when her husband began an affair with an English sculptress, Clare Sheridan, her political status remained intrinsically linked to that of her brother and her former husband, so that when they fell victim to Stalin, so did she. Kameneva's reputation has suffered a similar fate. For many historians, her contribution both to the Bolshevik Party and the Soviet government has been completely subsumed behind that of her famous husband and her more famous brother.

Larissa Reisner (1895-1926)

Larissa Reisner came to symbolise the heroic idealism of 1917. A generation younger than figures like Kollontai and Krupskaya, Reisner was a poet, revolutionary and fighter. She was one of the many young women who joined the Bolshevik Party in 1918 in order to defend the revolution from the White armies. Larissa Reisner became a military leader who also wrote acclaimed prose and poetic accounts of her experiences.

Reisner was born in 1895 in Lithuania to socialist parents who supported women's rights. She spent the first eight years of her life in Berlin, after the family fled there to avoid reprisals and pogroms. Her father joined the Bolshevik Party in 1905 and wrote articles for party publications. As a teenager, Reisner read Marx and Engels and many classics of Russian socialism and literature, and she began to write. In the summer of 1912, Larissa was 17 and a gold medal-winning student. With her family's help, she was allowed to enrol at the

University of St Petersburg and became well-known in pre-revolutionary St Petersburg as a writer. She was however appalled by the way many of her poetic heroes supported the First World War.

In 1916, Reisner took a steamer trip on the Volga with university friends. Her letters reveal her grasp of the revolution that was fermenting in the country. She wrote to her parents:

> *And another thing: we needn't fear for Russia. In the little sentry-boxes and market villages – along all the moorings of this vast river everything is irrevocably decided here they know everything, forgive nobody and forget nothing. And when the time comes, they will pass sentence and exact punishments such as have never before been seen. I am sometimes exhausted by helpless presentiments; if only the string doesn't snap too soon, if only these calm and terrible deeds don't remain mere words. But it's everywhere, beyond the yellowing forest edges, beyond the islands and rapids. And the elements are never mistaken.*[127]

After the February Revolution, Reisner became involved with Maxim Gorky's paper, *New Life*, and began teaching workers in the Provisional Government's spelling reform programme. 'It was Larissa's first experiences of meeting Petrograd's masses which formed her as a revolutionary and changed her life', wrote Cathy Porter.[128] In the sailors' clubs of Krondstadt, Reisner met the Bolshevik Fyodor Raskolnikov, whom she later married. Immediately after the October Revolution, Reisner went to the Bolshevik Central Committee to offer her services: 'I can ride, shoot, reconnoitre, write, send correspondence from the front, and, if necessary, die…'[129] She began to work with Anatoly Lunacharsky in the department for education.

In March 1918, some 50,000 Czech soldiers rose up against the Bolsheviks, Japanese troops invaded Russia and White armies financed by Britain, the US and France all waged war on the new regime. Reisner worked behind enemy lines, risking her life and witnessing many terrible scenes of suffering. She was active along the Volga River, near the town of Samara, where she carried out dangerous surveillance work. On her return to Petrograd in 1920 she wrote the hugely popular *Letters from the Front* which emphasised women's role in warfare. Reisner became the first Bolshevik female political commissar in the Red Army and during 1919 she served the Commissar at the Navel Staff HQ in Moscow.

Reisner and her husband were posted to Afghanistan in 1921 and lived there for two years. Reisner was given responsibility for winning Afghanistan to the Russian cause. In 1923, she travelled illegally into Germany where she witnessed the abortive German Revolution of 1923. At the height of her fame, she returned to Russia and travelled in the Ural Mountains where she described the hard life led by miners. Her writings were widely read and celebrated throughout Soviet Russia during the 1920s.

Reisner's most famous book was *The Front*, an account of her experiences during the Civil War. She wrote in a new, direct, literary style:

> *To fight for three years, to march with guns for thousands of miles to chew bread made with straw, to die, rot and shake with terror on a filthy bed in some flea-ridden hospital-and to conquer! Yes, to conquer the enemy who is three times stronger than we are, armed with our clapped-out rifles, our collapsing planes and our fourth-rate petrol, while all the time wretched, angry letters arrive for our loved ones at home... For all this, I think we need a few verbal outbursts, don't you?*[130]

A review of the book praised how, 'The author has, with exceptional talent, described how people made the

Revolution, and how the Revolution made them'.[131]

Reisner died of typhus in February 1926, aged just 30. It is a sad irony that today it is much easier to find the words of the men who paid tribute to this revolutionary woman writer than it is to find her own words. Reisner wrote little about the specific battles faced by women. As Cathy Porter explained, 'Larissa Reisner came of age at a time when it finally seemed possible for women to overstep the conventional female ethic of submission, renunciation and domesticity. Her writings vibrate with the power and challenge of women's life in the Revolution, and of the limitless possibilities, uncertainties and dangers opening up for them.'[132]

Anna Ulyanova

Nadezhda Krupskaya

Alexandra Kollontai

Elena Stasova

Inessa Armand

Konkordia Samoilova

Olga Kameneva

Larissa Reisner

Notes

1. Alexander Rabinovitch, *The Bolsheviks Come to Power*, (London, 2004), p.345.

2. Richard Stites, *The Women's Liberation Movement in Russia: Feminism, Nihilism and Bolshevism 1860-1930*, (Princetown, 1978), p.289.

3. China Miéville, *October: The Story of the Russian Revolution*, (London, 2017).

4. Tariq Ali, *The Dilemmas of Lenin: Terrorism, War, Empire, Love, Revolution*, (London, 2017).

5. Robert H McNeal, *Bride of the Revolution: Krupskaya and Lenin*, (Littlehampton, 1973).

6. Robert Service, *Lenin: A Biography*, (London, 2000), p.97.

7. Cathy Porter, *Alexandra Kollontai: A Biography*, (London, 1980).

8. Carolyn J Eichener, *Women in the Paris Commune: Surmounting the Barricades*, (Indiana, 2004), p.25.

9. Edith Thomas, *The Women Incendiaries: The Fantastic Story of the Women of the Paris Commune Who Took up Arms in the Fight for Liberty and Equality*, (New York, 1966), p.75.

10. Cathy Porter, *Fathers and Daughters: Russian Women in Revolution*, (London, 1976), p.121.

11. Thomas, *Women Incendiaries*, p.75.

12. Ibid., p.114.

13. Mary Gabriel, *Love and Capital: Karl and Jenny Marx and the Birth of a Revolution*, (New York, 2011), p.433.

14. Thomas, *Women Incendiaries*, p.70.

15. Vladimir Ilyich Lenin, *State and Revolution* (New York, 1932).

16. Porter, *Alexandra Kollontai*, p.87.

17. Porter, *Fathers and Daughters*, p.37.

18. Leon Trotsky, *Lenin*, (New York, 1925), *Lenin and Old*

Iskra, part I, https://www.marxists.org/.

19. Oscar Wilde, *Vera; or, The Nihilists* (London, 1902).

20. Ali, *The Dilemmas of Lenin*, p.113.

21. Barbara Evans Clements, *Bolshevik Women*, (Cambridge, 1997), p.25.

22. http://alphahistory.com/russianrevolution/bloody-sunday-petition-1905/ 'The Bloody Sunday Petition to the Tsar' (1905).

23. Porter, *Alexandra Kollontai*, p.91.

24. Ibid., p.89.

25. Ibid., p.86.

26. Ibid., p.94.

27. Jane McDermid and Anna Hillyer, *Midwives of the Revolution: Women Bolsheviks and Women Workers in 1917*, (London, 1994).

28. Ibid, p.62.

29. Vladimir Ilyich Lenin, 'The Two Tactics of Social Democracy in the Democratic Revolution', Chapter 13, (1906) https://www.marxists.org/.

30. Miéville, *October*, p.67.

31. Porter, *Alexandra Kollontai*, p.146.

32. Clements, *Bolshevik Women*, p.21.

33. R J Evans, *Comrades and Sisters: Feminism, Socialism and Pacifism in Europe 1870-1945*, (New York, 1997), p.76.

34. Katy Turton, 'Forgotten Lives: The Role of Anna, Ol'ga and Mariia Ulyanova in the Russian Revolution, 1864-1937', PhD thesis, theses.gla.ac.uk (2004).

35. Evans, *Comrades and Sisters*, p.131.

36. Quoted in RAJ Schlesinger, *Changing Attitudes in Soviet Russia: The Family*, (London, 1949), p.328.

37. Helen Rappaport, *Caught in the Revolution: Petrograd, 1917*, (London, 2016), p.37.

38. Ibid., p.35.

39. Ibid., p.45.

40. Ibid., p.122.

41. McDermid and Hillyar, *Midwives of the Revolution*, p.142.

42. Leon Trotsky, *History of the Russian Revolution*, (New York, 1932), Chapter 8, 'Who led the February Insurrection?', paragraph 1, https://www.marxists.org/.

43. Trotsky, *History of the Russian Revolution*, Chapter 8, 'Who led the February Insurrection?', paragraph 29, (New York, 1932), https://www.marxists.org/.

44. Ibid., paragraph 31.

45. Marcel Liebman, *Leninism under Lenin*, (London, 1980), p.117.

46. P Sorokin, *Leaves from a Russian Diary*, (London, 1950), p.3.

47. E N Burdzhalov, *Russia's Second Revolution: The February 1917 Uprising in Petrograd*, (Bloomington, 1987), p.112.

48. Ibid., p.105.

49. Ibid.

50. Ibid., p.106.

51. Ibid., p.107.

52. Ibid., p.107.

53. Ibid., p.115.

54. Rapport, *Caught in the Revolution*, p.145.

55. Clements, *Bolshevik Women*, p.122.

56. Porter, *Alexandra Kollontai*, p.242.

57. McDermid and Hillyar, *Midwives of the Revolution*, p.159.

58. Sarah Badcock, 'Women, Protest and Revolution: Soldiers' Wives in Russia 1917', *International Review of Social History*, April 2003, (Cambridge, 2003), p.11.

59. Miéville, *October*, p.94.

60. Rappaport, *Caught in the Revolution*, p.147.

61. Porter, *Alexandra Kollontai*, p.251.

62. Clements, *Bolshevik Women*, p.101.

63. Porter, *Alexandra Kollontai*, p.252.

64. Ibid., p253.

65. Badcock, 'Women, Protest and Revolution', p.27.

66. Badcock, 'Women, Protest and Revolution', p.23.

67. Ibid.

68. Porter, *Alexandra Kollontai*, p.251.
69. Badcock, 'Women, Protest and Revolution', pp.22-3.
70. Miéville, *October*, p.115.
71. Badcock, 'Women, Protest and Revolution', p.2.
72. McDermid and Hillyar, *Midwives of the Revolution*, p.163.
73. Ibid., p.165.
74. Clements, *Bolshevik Women*, p.105.
75. Ibid., p.133.
76. Ibid., p.132.
77. Ibid.
78. Ibid., p.200.
79. Porter, *Alexandra Kollontai*, p.268.
80. Ibid., pp.267-8.
81. Clements, *Bolshevik Women*, p.126.
82. McDermid and Hillyar, *Midwives of the Revolution*, p.71.
83. Bessie Beatty, *The Red Heart of Russia*, (New York, 1918), p.358.
84. Ibid., p.358.
85. Alexandra Kollontai, 'Letter to Dora Montefiore', 1921, paragraph 5, https://www.marxists.org/.
86. Clements, *Bolshevik Women*, pp.180-4.
87. Ibid., p.129.
88. Porter, *Alexandra Kollontai*, p.283.
89. Ali, *Dilemmas of Lenin*, p.273.
90. Miéville, *October*, p.122.
91. Ali, *Dilemmas of Lenin*, p.269.
92. See for example, Sheila Rowbotham, chapter 'If You Like Tobogganing: Women in Russia Before and After the Revolution', *Women, Resistance and Revolution: A History of Women and Revolution in the Modern World* (London, 1973).
93. R C Ellwood, *Inessa Armand: Revolutionary and Feminist*, (Cambridge, 1992) p.240.
94. Beatty, *The Red Heart of Russia*, p.380.
95. Larissa Vasilieva (editor), *Kremlin Wives*, (London,

1994), p.9.

96. Porter, *Alexandra Kollontai*, p.248.

97. Liebman, *Leninism*, p.131.

98. Rabinowitch, *The Bolsheviks Come to Power*, p.265.

99. Turton, *Forgotten Lives*, p.2.

100. Clements, *Bolshevik Women*, pp.56-7.

101. Ibid., p.105.

102. Turton, *Forgotten Lives*, p.23.

103. Quoted in Turton, *Forgotten Lives*, p.34.

104. Service, *Lenin*, p.447.

105. Ibid., p.84.

106. Quoted in Turton, *Forgotten Lives*, p.63.

107. Ibid., pp.126-7.

108. Ibid., p.68.

109. Ibid., pp.69-70.

110. Jane McDermid and Anya Hillyard, 'In Lenin's Shadow: Nadezhda Krupskaya and the Bolshevik Revolution'. In: *Reinterpreting Revolutionary Russia: Essays in Honour of James D White*, (New York, 2006) p.148.

111. McNeal, *Bride of the Revolution*, p.101.

112. Helen Rappaport, *Conspirator: Lenin in Exile*, (London, 2009), p.17.

113. McNeal, *Bride of the Revolution*, p.79.

114. Rapport, *Conspirator*, p.74.

115. Leon Trotsky, *My Life*, (New York, 1903), Chapter XII: The Party Congress and the Split, paragraph 5, https://www.marxists.org/.

116. McNeal, *Bride of the Revolution*, p.175.

117. Ibid., p.177.

118. Ibid., p.188.

119. There is a wonderful recording of Kollontai speaking on YouTube: Alexandra Kollontai a las trabajadoras, 1918, https://www.youtube.com/watch?v=qQzyheiNVuY.

120. Alexandra Kollontai, *Communism and the Family*, (Petrograd, 1920), paragraph 3, https://www.marxists.org/.

121. Alexandra Kollontai, 'On the History of the Movement

of Women Workers in Russia', 1919, paragraph 6, https://
www.marxists.org/.

122. Alexandra Kollontai, 'Sexual Relations and the
Class Struggle', (Russia, 1921), paragraph 7, https://www.
marxists.org/.

123. Rappaport, *Conspirator*, pp.190-4.

124. Ali, *Dilemmas of Lenin*, p.284.

125. Elwood, *Inessa Armand*, p.125.

126. Bertram D Woolfe, *Strange Communists I have known:
Inessa Armand*, (New York, 1965).

127. Cathy Porter, *Larissa Reisner*, (London, 1988) p.39.

128. Ibid., p.42.

129. Ibid., p.45.

130. Ibid., p.152.

131. Ibid., p.53.

132. Ibid., p.2.

Timeline

	Divorce made accessible
	Equal Pay legislation enacted
	Homosexuality legalised
1918	July: First Russian Constitution grants men and women equal rights
	November: First All-Women Congress meets
1919	*Zhenotdel* formed
1920	Abortion legalised
1967	Abortion legalised in Britain – but not in Northern Ireland
	Homosexuality decriminalised in Britain
1969	Divorce made accessible to women in UK
1970	Equal Pay Act, Britain

About the author

Judy Cox

Judy Cox is a lifelong socialist writer and speaker. Now a teacher in East London, Judy has written, amongst other things, on Marx's theory of alienation, Rosa Luxemburg's economic theory, William Blake and Robin Hood.

Acknowledgements

Many thanks to Elaine Graham-Leigh and Feyzi Ismail for all their help, support and advice.

Further reading

Tariq Ali, *The Dilemmas of Lenin: Terrorism, War, Empire, Love, Revolution* (Verso, 2017)

Sarah Badcock, 'Women, Protest and Revolution: Soldiers' Wives in Russia 1917' in *International Review of Social History*, April 2003 (Cambridge, 2003)

Carolyn J Eichener, *Women in the Paris Commune: Surmounting the Barricades* (Indiana, 2004)

Barbara Evans Clements, *Bolshevik Women* (Cambridge, 1997)

Jane McDermid and Anna Hillyer, *Midwives of the Revolution: Women Bolsheviks and Women Workers in 1917* (London, 1994)

Robert H McNeal, *Bride of the Revolution: Krupskaya and Lenin* (Littlehampton, 1973)

China Miéville, *October: The Story of the Russian Revolution* (Verso, 2017)

Cathy Porter, *Fathers and Daughters: Russian Women in Revolution* (London, 1976), *Alexandra Kollontai: A Biography* (London, 1980), *Larissa Reisner: A Biography* (London, 1988)

Alexander Rabinovitch, *The Bolsheviks Come to Power* (London, 2004)

Edith Thomas, *The Women Incendiaries: The Fantastic Story of the Women of the Paris Commune Who Took up Arms in the Fight for Liberty and Equality* (New York, 1966)

Katy Turton, *Forgotten Lives: The Role of Anna, Ol'ga and Mariia Ulyanova in the Russian Revolution, 1864-1937* (PhD thesis, available online at www.theses.gla.ac.uk, 2004)

About Haymarket Books

Haymarket Books is a radical, independent, nonprofit book publisher based in Chicago.

Our mission is to publish books that contribute to struggles for social and economic justice. We strive to make our books a vibrant and organic part of social movements and the education and development of a critical, engaged, international left.

We take inspiration and courage from our namesakes, the Haymarket martyrs, who gave their lives fighting for a better world. Their 1886 struggle for the eight-hour day—which gave us May Day, the international workers' holiday—reminds workers around the world that ordinary people can organize and struggle for their own liberation. These struggles continue today across the globe—struggles against oppression, exploitation, poverty, and war.

Since our founding in 2001, Haymarket Books has published more than five hundred titles. Radically independent, we seek to drive a wedge into the risk-averse world of corporate book publishing. Our authors include Noam Chomsky, Arundhati Roy, Rebecca Solnit, Angela Y. Davis, Howard Zinn, Amy Goodman, Wallace Shawn, Mike Davis, Winona LaDuke, Ilan Pappé, Richard Wolff, Dave Zirin, Keeanga-Yamahtta Taylor, Nick Turse, Dahr Jamail, David Barsamian, Elizabeth Laird, Amira Hass, Mark Steel, Avi Lewis, Naomi Klein, and Neil Davidson. We are also the trade publishers of the acclaimed Historical Materialism Book Series and of Dispatch Books.